Thus Says the Lord

Thus Says the Lord

Messages
From the
Minor
Prophets

Zdravko Stefanovic

REVIEW AND HERALD® PUBLISHING ASSOCIATION
Since 1861 | www.reviewandherald.com

This book was
Edited by Gerald Wheeler
Copyedited by Ted Hessel
Cover designed by Bryan Gray / Review and Herald® Design Center
Cover art © by Eric Stenbakken/Goodsalt.com
Interior designed by Emily Ford / Review and Herald® Design Center
Typeset: Minion Pro 11/13

PRINTED IN U.S.A.

16 15 14 13 12   5 4 3 2 1

Library of Congress Cataloging-in-Publication Data
Stefanovic, Zdravko.
 Thus says the Lord: messages from the minor prophets / Zdravko Stefanovic.
    p. cm.
  1. Bible. O.T. Minor Prophets—Criticism, interpretation, etc. I. Title.
BS1560.S74 2012
224'.906—dc23   2012016006

ISBN: 978-0-8280-2634-5

Dedication

This book is dedicated to my parents,
Milenko and Jozefina,
who showed me how to respect and love the
Bible with my whole being.

Contents

A Map of the Kingdoms of Israel and Judah

SYRIA

PHOENICIA

Tyre

Dan

GREAT SEA

Sea of Chinnereth

Ramoth

Megiddo

Beth-shean

● ISRAEL

Samaria

Shiloh

Bethel

Jericho

AMMON

Ekron

Jerusalem

Tekoa

Gaza

PHILISTIA

Hebron

En-gedi

Salt Sea

Beersheba

JUDAH

Kir of Moab

MOAB

Kadesh-barnea

EGYPT

EDOM

Bible History Online

Introduction

The Book of the Twelve Prophets

A Jewish rabbi often told his followers: "Repent one day before you die!" The question that would immediately follow was "How can I know when I will die?" The teacher answered by saying: "You cannot know that; therefore, repent every day!" Biblical prophets were men and women sent by God to call the people to repent or to come back to their Lord and to the teaching He had revealed through His servant Moses. The messages they proclaimed originated in the loving heart of God. The prophets' task was not only to comfort the weak, but also to confront the sins of idolatry and social oppression. They exhorted the people to renounce their evil ways so that the Lord could truly bless them and their land.

The Book of the Twelve Prophets

A common way of referring to the last 12 books of the Old Testament in modern editions of the Bible is the minor prophets. The word "minor" comes from Latin and means "smaller." It distinguishes the collection of these books from the four major prophets: Isaiah, Jeremiah, Ezekiel, and Daniel. We need to point out, however, that the 12 prophetic books are minor, not in their importance, but in their individual sizes. Indeed, we can find a great number of major lessons within the books of the minor prophets.

Since the word "minor" designating a prophetic book does not appear in the Bible, some scholars rightly argue that we should consider it as a misnomer and avoid it altogether. The Jews and early Christians referred to these books as the Book of the Twelve. They treated the collection of all 12 documents as a single scroll or one book. In this way, their total length matched that of Isaiah, Jeremiah, or Ezekiel.

Although seemingly lost in the mists of time, biblical prophets were real people who addressed actual life situations. They preached their messages before anyone wrote them down. The voices resounding from their books appear, at times, angry and even judgmental. While they tear down a facade of pretended piety, yet at the same time they build a strong structure of faith that rests on God's compassion and mercy. Divine purpose has preserved the messages of the prophets for our instruction so that today an even wider audience than originally intended by their authors can still appreciate them.

The prophets were well aware of human sinfulness and of God's coming punishment. They were equally aware of His generous offer of forgiveness if people repent. Being close to God, they knew well the "anger and frustration, awe and anguish, hope and despair, but they also knew a God of uncompromising holiness, irrevocable justice and inexhaustible love and mercy."[1] Their messages of judgment and salvation ring down the centuries to our times with an incredible force.

As spokespersons for God, biblical prophets were primarily preachers or forthtellers of the messages entrusted to them. They called the people back to their God and the covenant He had made with them long before. The prophets were reformers of the faith whose roots go back to the experiences of the patriarchs and matriarchs. "Their call to reform is not radical in the sense of being new, rather it is radical because the people have strayed so far from God."[2] Such reform, they taught, leads to blessings and renewed hope.

The prophets were also announcers or foretellers of future events related to God's plan of salvation. Some of the predictions recorded in their books speak of the judgments that would occur in the near future. Others pertain to a distant time in which God would usher in His kingdom and when the faithful from all parts of the globe will be restored and dwell forever with their Lord. Thus when they spoke of a distant future, the prophets did so in order to urge people to reform their lives in the present.

The 12 prophets lived, ministered, and wrote their words from the eighth down to the fifth centuries B.C. Their messages embrace all the major themes found in Scripture, climaxing in the announcement of the day of the Lord and the coming of the promised Messiah. Although the order in which we find their books in our Bible is not strictly chronological, their ministries belong to the era of the Assyrian, Neo-Babylonian, and Medo-Persian empires.

What were some of the problems that the prophets addressed so boldly? In the first place, it was the people's unfaithfulness to their God, an attitude that resulted in growing disparity between the rich and poor with the injustice that went along with it. The worship activities in the Temple were only a cover-up for a superficial faith in God. Society valued prosperity more than righteousness. Both people and leaders claimed to be religious, but they did not know the Lord. The prophets boldly proclaimed that such sins as corruption, robbery, murder, and other vices break not just God's law but also His heart.

After a careful reading and study of the books of the 12 prophets, the reader is able to see that the passing centuries have not dimmed their power of prophetic proclamation. Instead, they continue to speak out with vigor and irresistible influence. The reader cannot help becoming once more astonished and even transformed by the influence of the same Spirit that long ago inspired the human authors of these ancient documents, a process aptly expressed in the following statement: "Through nature, through types and symbols, through patriarchs and prophets, God had spoken to the world. Lessons must be given to humanity in the language of humanity. . . . The principles of God's government and the plan of redemption must be clearly defined. The lessons of the Old Testament must be fully set before men."[3]

The Ministry of Biblical Prophets

In any study of biblical prophecy it is essential to begin with a description of the person holding the prophetic office. The community knew such individuals by several titles, such as "seer," "prophet," "spokesman for God," or simply "man of God." Prophets were, in the first place, spiritual leaders of the community to which they ministered. It is remarkable that we find the very first occurrence of the word "prophet" in the Bible in a context of prayer and healing (Gen. 20:6, 7). The prophets did not choose their occupation—God called them to be His spokespersons. Their task consisted of proclaiming God's messages to the people of their time, as well as pointing to God's future dealings with His people and with the nations of the world.

We may divide the Hebrew prophets into two groups: the writing and nonwriting prophets. Most of the messages delivered by the earliest prophets in Israel were oral and probably never written down. The recorded messages of biblical prophets, on the other hand, served as a reliable witness to their listeners and readers, showing that God is just and merciful in dealing with His people and with the non-Israelite nations. Scholars generally classify the written oracles of the prophets into three groups: (1) local or immediate; (2) end-time (eschatological), either national or universal; (3) apocalyptic or cosmic. Apocalyptic prophecy is universal in scope and it "celebrates God's victory over the enemies of the godly," because His people are oppressed and persecuted in the present age. Although apocalyptic predictions appear to be deterministic, the reader of the Bible should not lose sight of the fact that the ultimate goal of *all* prophecy, including apocalyptic, is repentance and the salvation of human beings.

The prophetic utterances in the Bible did not occur in a vacuum, but were rather grounded in history. For that reason it is important to study the original context in which we find a prophecy. An important point of biblical teaching is that God's past and present leading either in the life of a group of people or that of an individual will provide landmarks for the future. An example from the Song at the Sea (Ex. 15) will illustrate this. The Israelites have just witnessed God's power at work as He defeated the Egyptians who had been pursuing them. Their enemy has "sank to the depths like a stone" (verse 5). As they sing a hymn of praise to God (verses 1-12), their eyes of faith turn away from the sea toward the Promised Land (verse 13). The second part of their song proclaims that the same God who had just delivered them from their enemies will lead them safely to the land of Canaan (verses 17, 18). Should any people attempt to stand in the way, God will deal with their army in the same way as He did with the Egyptians (verses 14-16). The song says that by the power of God's arm future enemies "will be as still as a stone" (verse 16). Thus we may define the future in terms of biblical prophecy as a continuation of God's past leading but in an ever more powerful way as the end draws near.

Generally speaking, biblical prophecy is the sum of divine revelations that disclose both God's present dealings with the world and His ultimate goal of saving repentant humanity. The Hebrew prophets made predictions which they claimed originated with God. Thus they form an essential part of biblical prophecy, and their fulfillments attest to the fact that the persons who made them were true prophets (Deut. 18:21, 22; Jer. 14; Eze. 13). Yet predictions are only one part of biblical prophecy. This is the reason that we should never restrict biblical prophecies just to the level of announcing future events. Some predictions are conditional, but prophecy as a whole is not. A prediction may not come to pass and may even seem to have failed, although divine prophecy never fails, because its ultimate goal is God's salvation of human beings. The prophet Isaiah described the effect of the prophetic word in the following way: "So is my word that goes out from my mouth: It will not return to me empty, but will accomplish what I desire and achieve the purpose for which I sent it" (Isa. 55:11).

Since God's redeeming purpose culminates in the person and work of the Messiah, all biblical prophecy in one way or another points to Jesus Christ. In this sense, our Savior is the ultimate fulfillment of prophecy, a truth that we can experience only when He reigns in our hearts. As God long ago moved the apostle Peter to say: "We also have the prophetic message as something completely reliable, and you will do well to pay attention to it, as to a light shining in a dark place, until the day dawns and the morning star rises in your hearts" (2 Peter 1:19).

---

[1] Harry Young, *Major Themes From Minor Prophets* (Grantham, Eng.: Autumn House, 1996), p. 12.

[2] Jon L. Dybdahl, *Hosea-Micah: A Call to Radical Reform* (Boise, Idaho: Pacific Press Pub. Assn., 1996), p. 23.

[3] Ellen G. White, *The Desire of Ages* (Mountain View, Calif.: Pacific Press Pub. Assn., 1898), p. 34.

Chapter 1

Messages From the Book of Hosea

While teaching in Asia, I was privileged to have Rob in my classes. For a number of years the man had been imprisoned because of his faith during a time of severe religious persecution in which many people died. Rob credits his resilience and miraculous survival to God, whose abiding presence he felt around him, and also to his wife who, throughout their long trial, remained faithful to her marriage vow. She patiently hoped and waited for the time the two of them would reunite. In contrast to her steadfast commitment stands the behavior of Gomer, who, according to the book of Hosea, left her husband in pursuit of lovers. Because Gomer was an Israelite, the story of her marriage to the prophet Hosea blends with that of God's covenant to Israel. The two narratives are essentially one. As a scholar aptly said, Hosea's marriage was "a historical reality with symbolic meaning."[1]

Hosea ministered at the close of a very prosperous period in Israel's history, shortly before the fall of the northern kingdom to the Assyrians in 722 B.C. At that time, God's chosen people no longer worshiped the Lord alone, but also served Baal, the Canaanite storm god believed to grant fertility. Shrines dedicated to idols dotted the landscape of the countryside. Placed at the head of the Twelve Prophets, the book of Hosea addresses the central question of the prophetic proclamation: Does God still love Israel? Does the Lord still have a purpose for His people in spite of their sins and the coming judgment? What has happened to the "covenant of love" (Deut. 7:9) between God and Israel? Hosea's book deals with these difficult issues and dilemmas. It clearly teaches that sin does not only break God's law, it also shatters His heart.

A Strange Command

Hosea's book opens with a surprising command from God to the prophet to marry Gomer, a woman who later proved unfaithful to her husband: "Go, marry a promiscuous woman and have children with her, for like an adulterous wife this land is guilty of unfaithfulness to the Lord" (Hosea 1:2). Scholars have debated the exact nature of the command. Some have argued that the Lord told the prophet to marry a woman who was already immoral, while others have maintained that Gomer became unfaithful only after her marriage to Hosea.

We cannot be sure that Hosea intended to provide us with precise answers to such questions when he wrote the book. Whichever position we might take, God's action appears extreme, because nowhere else in the Bible do we find recorded that the Lord issued a similar command. What is certain from Hosea's book is that God was determined to get His point across to Israel—even if He had to direct one of His servants to share in His own experience.

Not only Hosea's marriage but also the children born to him were signs of how God related to Israel. The names given to Gomer's three children were symbolic of the Lord's reproof of His people: *Jezreel*, or "God will scatter," points to the prospect of captivity to a foreign country. Just as Jehu had put an end to Ahab's house, so would a foreign nation totally eliminate Israel's kingship and nationhood. The second name, *Lo-Ruhama*, or "no compassion," negates the most important trait of God's character as revealed to Moses on Mount Sinai: "The Lord, the Lord, the compassionate and gracious God, slow to anger, abounding in love and faithfulness" (Ex. 34:6). God will show no pity to those who exchange His glory for idols. The third name, *Lo-Ammi*, or "not my people," reverses God's unique way of addressing Israel, the Lord's firstborn child, blessed with special privileges and responsibilities. Thus Hosea gave each child born to Gomer a prophetic name in order to teach his fellow Israelites that the next generation would be burdened by their parents' rejection of loyalty and devotion to God.

Hosea's marriage served as an object lesson intended to show the breaking of the covenant between God and Israel. A man in ancient Israel would have had to make a tremendous effort to forgive and take back an unfaithful wife, not to mention to accept as his own children who may have been fathered by another man. To stand by his wife and her children and thus endure social rejection would be one of the most difficult life experiences of the time. Yet that is precisely what the God of love was willing to do for unfaithful Israel. His ultimate purpose was to illustrate His redemptive act toward sinners. A ray of hope was still shining through the darkness of the coming judgment. For this reason, the first chapter of Hosea's book closes with a promise that, in the end, the Lord would restore and bless His people by making them once again the object of His special love and care.

The promises made to the ancestors long ago (Gen. 22:17, 18) could still be fulfilled: "Yet the Israelites will be like the sand on the seashore, which cannot be measured or counted. In the place where it was said to them, 'You are not my people,' they will be called 'children of the living God'" (Hosea 1:10). Israel's divided kingdom would be reunited by a David-like king. The names of the children would be changed in order to fit the new situation: *Jezreel*, or "God will scatter," would become *Jezreel*, meaning "God will plant."[2] Also, *Lo-Ruhama*, or "no compassion," would become *Ruhama*, or "the beloved." Finally, *Lo-Ammi*, or "not my people," would become *Ammi*, or "the people (of the living God)."

The prophet's behavior raised many questions for the people. At times they may have wondered about his sanity. But Hosea knew that God had commanded him to act inexplicably, no matter what questions it might lead to. Symbolically, they were God's vital method to get across His message to those who would see and hear it. Through words of warning and hope, God wooed His people to return to Him and thus avoid the destruction their actions had made inevitable.

God's Broken Heart

The dominant themes of Hosea's prophecy are faithfulness and unfaithfulness. The Bible views idolatry as spiritual adultery. Just as Gomer broke Hosea's heart by defiling herself with other men, so Israel grieved God by polluting itself with idol worship. Hosea 2 begins with words of dispute and judgment because the Lord's faithless wife has deserted Him and needs to be betrothed to Him again. When Gomer proved unfaithful to Hosea, he felt heartbroken, betrayed, and distraught. Yet the more he experienced Gomer's unfaithfulness, the deeper was his understanding of God's pain and frustration with Israel. Based on his personal experience, the prophet reminded the people that they were a nation bound to God through a special covenant relationship. This meant that Israel was not in control of its destiny. Being a special nation, it was not free to choose its gods or observe its own standards of behavior.

From the very beginning the Lord intended marriage to be a lasting commitment of love. Adultery violates the purpose of the sacred institution. Hosea taught that in a spiritual sense, God and Israel were husband

and wife. By being unfaithful to their Lord, the people were committing adultery with "lovers." The people had taken the gifts of God's blessing and presented them in their idol worship: "She has not acknowledged that I was the one who gave her the grain, the new wine and oil, who lavished on her the silver and gold—which they used for Baal" (Hosea 2:8). The nation was guilty of the worst type of spiritual adultery.

In an effort to dissuade Gomer from her persistent unfaithfulness, the prophet announces the reproach that she deserves. Similarly, the nation of Israel would be judged because of its apostasy and infidelity. Its punishment in the wilderness will prepare Israel for a renewed relationship with God. The Lord must show Israel that its infidelity is wrong.

Israel's blessings of prosperity had been a gracious manifestation of God's love. Since Israel's economy was agricultural, its society was extremely rain conscious. In Hosea's time people believed that Baal sent rain to earth.[3] But Hosea taught that Baal was not the source of blessings—rather, it was the Lord. In order to teach them this important lesson, God would allow Israel to be deprived of grain, new wine, oil, wool, and flax (verse 9). Moreover, the Lord would lay the nation bare, and in doing so shame her before her lovers. All occasions of joy and gladness would vanish from the land. The loss of all its blessings would finally make the people realize the true identity of their generous Provider.

A Second Honeymoon

The message of hope in Hosea's book reveals that the harsh punishment was not an end in itself, but rather paved the way for a rekindled romance. After all, one cannot build a true relationship on the basis of punishment. Thus the second half of chapter 2 portrays a future time beyond judgment, when God would woo Israel to sing again a love song to Him "as in the days of her youth, as in the day she came up out of Egypt" (verse 15). The original word for "allure" or "woo" connotes enticement and seduction (cf. Judges 16:5; Prov. 1:10). The revitalized relationship between the Lord and His people will be tender and intimate. God will no longer be someone detached and far off.

Out of pure and unfailing love, God had established the covenant that made Israel His special people (Ex. 15:13). That same love would be the basis for reestablishing the covenant with all its blessings. But how would this surprising turn of events take place? The prophet said that when God hems His unfaithful spouse in on every side, she would fail to find her lovers. Her disappointment would lead to a desire to return to her true husband with whom she "was better off than now" (Hosea 2:7). Thus the prophet makes the daring claim that God chooses to court Israel again in order to win her away from foreign gods.

The Lord sounds nostalgic for the days of Israel's wandering in the wilderness prior to the time when they were tempted into the worship of Baal in the land of Canaan. The expression "into the wilderness" (verse 14) sounds much like the Hebrew title for the book of Numbers,[4] which describes God's experiences with Israel in the desert. In this solitary place, where they will be alone, dwelling "in tents" (Hosea 12:9), God will speak tenderly or "to the heart" of His people (cf. Ruth 2:13; Isa. 40:2). No longer will God threaten to make Israel "like a desert, turn her into a parched land, and slay her with thirst" (Hosea 2:3). Instead, the Lord will show love to His people after their punishment and judgment.

Following the renewal and restoration of relations, the Lord will give back all that He took away from His people during the time of punishment. "The reconciliation will take effect as a new betrothal. And these will be the gift and dowry for the bride: righteousness, justice, kindness, mercy. The pathos of love, expressed first in the bitterness and disillusionment, finds its climax in the hope of reconciliation."[5] God will demonstrate to His people that His love is better than that of false gods can ever be. The broken family will be restored to wholeness forever, pointing to the stability of the renewed relationship. Fairness, dependable love, faithfulness, and compassion will now characterize Israel's society. Moreover, the restored relationship will affect all creation. The earth will be blessed, peace will replace war and destruction, and harmony will prevail in nature. God will have finally realized His plan of healing and reconciliation for all of His creatures. All of creation celebrates while heaven and earth rejoice (Hosea 2:21, 22).

This powerful prophetic passage contains some timeless lessons for living. It teaches that whatever the source of our suffering might be, it can lead us to seek God's help. All of us have hard times in our lives when we feel estranged from Him. "We all have wilderness experiences in which, even if we aren't being punished, we feel abandoned, or at least distant from God. Hosea says that God comes to that wilderness to win us back."[6] Once we have renewed our relationship with Him, the impact of this change will have far-reaching consequences, not just for us, but for everyone and everything that surrounds us.

The Unchanging Love

Hosea was not a mere messenger for God. He was also the message and the sign. His own life filled with pain and hope was a powerful sermon preached day by day to all who would listen and see. Oftentimes in the Bible the prophetic message became a living word for the prophets because God asked them to do something beyond preaching. He summoned the messenger to live out the meaning and the results of the divine message. Thus the prophetic actions symbolized God's future dealings with His people. Isaiah walked half-naked and barefoot for three years (Isa. 20:1-6) to illustrate Egypt's exile to Assyria. He and his family were "signs and symbols in Israel" (Isa. 8:18). Jeremiah once carried a wooden yoke on his neck (Jer. 27:2), while God told Ezekiel to grieve quietly over the sudden death of his wife (Eze. 24:16).

In the beginning of chapter 3 the prophet returns to his own marriage situation that was an analogy for God and Israel. Hosea is to go out, search for, and retrieve his immoral wife so that the nation would clearly know that the Lord still loves His own spiritually unfaithful spouse. Though the text does not state the name of the woman, most interpreters understand her to be Gomer. Hosea redeemed his wife from a desperate condition into which she had fallen. The total amount that Hosea paid to redeem her was in ancient Israel equal to what one offered as compensation for the loss of a household servant (Ex. 21:32). It appears that Hosea did not have enough "cash on hand," so he decided to empty the storeroom of his house in order to buy Gomer back (Hosea 3:2). It reveals a definite determination on his part to redeem the unfaithful spouse from a situation from which she could not extricate herself. It is likely that Gomer had fallen into some type of debt slavery and was in desperate need of redemption.

An indefinite period of segregation is imposed, and its purpose is to lead to Gomer's (and Israel's) purification and renewal. The nation would be deprived of all things that had led them away from the true God. The list begins with unfaithful leaders and goes on to sacrifices to other gods, pagan shrines, and certain household items that had been Israel's stumbling blocks. The Lord will do this purging out of His love and support for His chosen people so that they may be fully restored to Him after a period of captivity. Then the ideal leader will emerge from the dynasty of King David, and he will rule over the entire kingdom of the Lord.

The message of Hosea 1-3 is the truth about God's steadfast love for an undeserving people. The Lord's "love is not based on how the object of love responds. Rather, it comes in spite of what the beloved does!"[7] His longing for reunion and his hope for people's return is stronger than his feelings of jealousy.[8] The Lord keeps on loving because He is faithful to His promises. Like many other biblical prophets, Hosea teaches that God's love and faithfulness toward His people are timeless and constant. But better than any other prophet, Hosea "shows how God *feels*. In other parts of the Bible, God bares His powerful arm in action; He bares His mind as He reveals His thoughts. But here in Hosea, He bares His *heart* so we can sense how He feels."[9]

The story of Hosea's marriage and family life served as the platform for the prophetic message that the Israelites needed to hear. The prophet's own suffering because of Gomer and their children provided unparalleled insight into the heart of the Lord. Yet it is amazing to see how the story veils the details of the prophet's inner life. The prophet's acts and deeds are entirely in focus but not his emotional responses. This shows that the book is not about Hosea and his family, but about God and His people. The Word of God came to the people through the record of the prophet's life experience as it revealed perverse human behavior and betrayal, resulting in divine outrage, suffering, compassion, and unchanging love.[10]

God Takes Israel to Court

Hosea 4 offers a summary of the entire book's prophetic message. It begins a long indictment on the morally corrupt, politically decaying, and spiritually dead nation presented from God's point of view. The prophet boldly states that the land is full of lying, stealing, adultery, and bloodshed. All of nature suffers the tragic consequences of human sins. The beasts of the field, the birds of the sky, and the fish of the sea have felt the impact of corruption. "Human wickedness pollutes nature and all the creatures within it. This cosmic corruption is described as a drought. The land dries up, the inhabitants languish, and creatures perish."[11]

As spokesperson for God, Hosea brings charges, one after another, against unfaithful people. The original word for "a charge" (Hosea 4:1) can also mean "a dispute" or a "lawsuit." In other words, the nation stands guilty before God. Israelite society lacked some of the key qualities in Israel's relationship with the Lord, such as faithfulness and steadfast love. Hosea courageously proclaimed that the nation's failure to know God had resulted in many sins. In ancient Israel it was the duty of the priests to teach people the knowledge of God. Yet the descendants of Aaron had failed to instruct others, resulting in Israel's corruption and leading to the rejection of divine teaching and worship, harlotry, and divine punishment described in the chapter.

The setting for Hosea's speech may have been one of the royal shrines located in the two border cities Bethel and Dan (cf. Amos 7). The prophet strongly denounced Israel's leaders, the foremost of whom were immoral priests (Hosea 4) and princes (Hosea 5, NASB) who shared in the current deterioration of religious life and would be held accountable for it. The priests and prophets who officiated in these illegitimate shrines could stumble at any time, both at night when people expected a disaster to strike, and in daytime when one usually felt safe. This would lead to the destruction of the nation, here personified as "mother" (Hosea 4:5). Thus the collapse of Israel's key ministers of God's Word will inevitably lead to disaster and tragedy.

The knowledge that people lacked included the recognition of the one God of Israel, what He had done for the people, and what He required in return. The people's ignorance of His will had resulted from the priest's rejection of the knowledge of God, and that would, in turn, lead to the Lord's removal of the priesthood. Moreover, since the priest has forgotten the divine instruction, God threatens to forget his sons who would normally inherit his priestly office. Instead of leading people away from sin toward the Lord, the priests subsist off the people's transgressions.

The increase of sin in the nation was in proportion to the prosperity of the land. So the Lord threatens to transform material prosperity into disgrace. People's lust for the fruit of the vine takes away their understanding. Turning to the wooden cult objects of the goddess Asherah in search of revelation (verse 12), they spurn true prophecy. They worship Baal on elevated sites that the people deem sacred. Under the shade of trees, the daughters of priests practice immorality. Since the priests lack spiritual understanding, the people can no longer discern between good and evil. Both priests and people have turned away from the knowledge of God and have made shameful idols for their empty worship.

Hosea joins Amos in urging people to abandon their customary cultic pilgrimages to the shrines in Gilgal and Bethel (verse 15). He changes the name Bethel, or "House of God," to Beth Aven, or "House of Sin." Employing images of agricultural and pastoral wildlife, the prophet mocks Israel's folly (verse 16). He asks a rhetorical question: Does a stubborn cow deserve the gentle treatment of a lamb? Hosea's favorite way to refer to the northern kingdom of Israel is Ephraim (verse 17), the name of Joseph's younger son who became Jacob's adopted son. Sadly, the tribe of Ephraim later became foremost in idolatrous practices in Israel (Ps. 78:56-67).

In chapter 5 Hosea presents charges against the "house of the king" or the ruling family in the capital city of Samaria who sponsored the idolatrous shrines and their personnel. Sadly, those same leaders failed to enforce justice in the land. Instead of depending on God, Israel chose self-reliance because of pride (Hosea 5:5). Once God brings devastation on the fields, it will put Baal to shame and his worshippers will be stripped of the crops that clothed and fed the people (verse 7). Although severe in nature, the divine judgment sought not just to lay waste to the kingdom but to drive people to repentance.

In his role as the nation's watchman, the prophet shouts a cry of warning announcing the approaching battle. Three towns located north of Jerusalem will come under attack first. The war will reduce Israel's territory to a small remnant because the leaders practiced oppression and social injustice. The calamities resulting from the war will include all sorts of pestilences. Both the kingdoms of Ephraim and Judah will seek help from the foreign nations of Aram and Assyria instead of placing their trust in God (verses 12-15). But those nations could not offer a lasting balm for the ailments of God's people. God intends His divine judgment to lead them to repentance and a sincere seeking of Him.

The messages found in these two chapters of Hosea are very clear: along with the privileges and honor enjoyed by powerful leaders come enormous responsibilities. Although power of itself is neutral, it is relational and open to abuse and corruption. Hosea says that God holds doubly accountable those individuals who hold spiritual offices. Their lives should never become devoid of divine presence.

A Call to Return

The word "return" appears frequently in Hosea, and it can also describe conversion or repentance. The book presents the themes of both human repentance and divine forgiveness and mercy. The purpose of divine judgment was to remind sinners that their life and strength derive from God to whom they must return. The prophet invites Israel to come back to the Lord and, in doing so, he includes himself in the act of submission to divine discipline. He proposes the very words that the people would employ at the time of their return. God, whom he has previously pictured as a lion tearing and carrying off (verse 14), the prophet now presents as powerful to bind up and heal His wounded people speedily (Hosea 6:1, 2). This intervention anticipates the national resurrection after death in exile, with the individual physical resurrection of the faithful included (cf. Isa. 26; Eze. 37; Dan. 12:2). Several New Testament passages apply this text to Jesus Christ's resurrection (Luke 24:46; 1 Cor. 15:4).

Unfortunately, the Lord's complaint that Ephraim's loyalty and love are comparable to a fleeting cloud and evaporating dew, both of which vanish with sunrise (Hosea 6:4), now dashes all hope that Israel will come back to Him. Instead of steadfast love, the winds of promiscuity blow in the land. The prophet expresses the divine judgments with past tense verbs to stress their certainty. Although the prophecy describes the future, God's Word is already as good as done. In contrast with people's transitory nature, it is as dependable as daybreak.

Like other biblical prophets,[12] Hosea pictures the quest for God's approval through animal sacrifices as vain (Hosea 6:6). Obedience and covenantal loyalty do not accompany the offering. People and leaders have forgotten that obedience is more important than sacrifice. The Lord will not let those who disobey Him to manipulate Him.[13] God Himself witnesses the crimes of the nation. They include acts of ambush—murders committed by gangs of priests on the Shechem Road. Yet God longs to show mercy to His people. While His gracious intention embraces the whole nation, corruption and iniquity block it, leading to destructive consequences. Hosea 6 teaches that the spiritual healing process has two aspects: repentance and faith. Israel in Hosea's time did not exhibit either of the two because of the hypocrisy that had infected sacrificial offerings. In addressing the Pharisees on one occasion, Jesus quoted Hosea 6:6, saying: "I desire mercy, not sacrifice" (Matt. 9:13). "A ritual that does not celebrate a repentant and healed life is meaningless."[14]

Like a Silly Dove

The Lord greatly desires to heal Ephraim in order to restore the nation's fortunes. To "heal" is one of the prophet's favorite terms for the reversal of Israel's unfaithfulness and consequent suffering in judgment (Hosea 5:13; 6:1; 11:3; 14:4). But the people's sinful conduct—led by the elite from the capital city of Samaria—block God's gracious plan to restore the nation. Even the spiritual leaders behaved as though God no longer held them accountable for their conduct. The prophet discloses the priestly participation in the treason against the ruling king. Hosea also indicts the princes because of their role in the wicked folly of Israel's court (Hosea 7:3). Those who should have protected the king's life left him defenseless and thus ready to be consumed in the hot oven of conspiracy. Repeatedly Hosea uses the oven metaphor to describe the ambitious passions of the priests (verses 4, 6, 7). Although the situation in the land is critical, no leader calls on the Lord for help. Instead, they continue on their own, ignoring what God alone can do.

Chapter 8 expands the theme of Israel's unfaithfulness to the Lord. Traditional Jewish interpreters associated the picture of the "eagle" with King Nebuchadnezzar (Eze. 17) who destroyed the Jerusalem Temple. As a metaphor of strength and speed, the eagle may also symbolize other invading armies such as Assyria. The prophet's duty is to sound an alarm to alert the people just as ancient Israel blew a shofar (ram's horn) in times of national crisis. The final 25 years of the northern kingdom witnessed a rapid succession of rulers whom the prophet considers illegitimate kings (Hosea 8:4-6). God's judgment would target illicit national leaders who made fruitless foreign alliances (verses 7-10) and worshiped idols.

Hosea's text provides numerous metaphors of judgment: a hot oven (Hosea 7:1-7), a half-baked bread (verses 8-10), a silly dove (verses 11-13), a defective bow (verses 14-16), futile farming (Hosea 8:7), a useless pot (verse 8), a wild donkey (verse 9), etc. The messages of divine revelation employed everyday experiences from life. Half-baked bread is one example that illustrates Ephraim's overcommitment to the surrounding nations and its rather weak commitment to God. The flat disk of dough shaped like pita bread was, in this case, left unturned by the baker, so it ended up being raw on the one side and scorched on the other.

Since Ephraim's foreign policy was not well thought out, the prophet compared the nation to a senseless dove devoid of judgment. The various political factions sought to gain power or protection through the aid of foreign countries. But such political gamesmanship could never be a lasting solution to Israel's problems. An alliance with the mighty Assyrian empire or ambitious Egypt would require Israel to recognize the supremacy of the gods worshipped by those superpowers. The Bible considers such a thing as an act of rebellion against God. In response, the Lord, portrayed as a crafty cosmic hunter, will spread His net over the wayward people and catch them. Later the image reverses when God's people return home as trembling birds (Hosea 11:11).

Human beings have always been tempted to worship on their own terms, not God's. Like many people in ancient Israel, today we can appear increasingly pious while at the same time we keep on worshipping idols. This is why Hosea uses terrifying metaphors to show that God's retribution is inevitable on those who serve Him with a divided heart. It requires personal decisions in order to reform one's life. God rejects all external signs of religiosity without genuine conversion (Hosea 6:6; 8:13). Hearts have to be transformed and then immersed in the steadfast love and the knowledge of the Lord. The same God who brings punishment is the only one who can heal and bind up spiritual wounds.

Finding Grapes in the Wilderness

The prophet proclaimed the command "Do not rejoice, O Israel!" (Hosea 9:1, NRSV) during the Feast of Tabernacles, a joyous occasion that celebrated both the fall harvest and looked back to the wilderness period of Israel's history. A sentence of exile that would make all religious festivities impossible (verses 3-5) immediately follows the command not to rejoice. Idolatry has tainted the Lord's land. The more bountiful its crops, the more convinced the people became in the rightness of their religious practices. The sight of overflowing threshing floors and wine vats seemed to affirm their conviction. But Hosea warns that the invading army will devour the food supply. Those who try to flee before the destruction of the cruel Assyrians will not find respite. To their surprise, they will be collected, die, and be buried in Egypt, a land that does not lack graveyards.

Hosea not only announces that judgment is certainly coming but states that it is in fact already here. But instead of admitting their guilt, Hosea's audience responds to his message with anger. Deep within their hearts, the people know that the prophet is right. But some regarded him as a fool in order to discredit his ministry (verse 7). Generally speaking, no prophet enjoyed a life of ease in Bible times. They had the courage to address the contemporary situation and unmask religious and social evils. The prophets warned that there would be catastrophic consequences if the leaders' present course should continue. As a result, people did not welcome what they said, and it usually fell on deaf ears. The prophet is, in the end, rejected by the majority of the people. Thus the coming of the divine judgment becomes inevitable.

Hosea borrows several metaphors from agricultural and pastoral activities and uses them to describe Israel's past relationship with God and the tragic reversal that had taken place. The prophet portrays the Lord as a farmer who is "tender with the crops and flocks, eager for their produce, frustrated by the failure, drastic in his means of correcting the problems."[15] God speaks fondly of the past history when He says that He was joyfully surprised to find refreshing, juicy fruit in an unlikely place such as the wilderness. At that time, He delighted in Israel's great potential for fruitfulness (verse 10). Later, however, the fruit turned sour. The pristine innocence gave way to corruption. Baal-Peor, a place located at the threshold of the Promised Land, became a byword for Israel's shame.

As in the past, Ephraim's future will be equally fruitless, symbolized as without birth, pregnancy, or conception. The coming punishment will include the loss of children by premature death. Like the Canaanites, Israel will be driven from the same land because of their assimilation of Canaanite practices. The Lord will banish His unfaithful spouse. A permanent withdrawal of God's love with no future renewal in view now threatens the nation. Since the people have treasured worthless idols, they themselves will become worthless, losing that which is of matchless value. The Israelites are destined to become wanderers among the nations of the world whose practices they have made their own way of life.

The metaphor of the vine used in the beginning of chapter 10 builds on the picture of the grapes described as found by God in the wilderness (Hosea 9). Israel, like a vine, took root in Canaan and flourished (cf. Ps. 80:8-11; Isa. 5:1-7; Jer. 2:21; Eze. 17:5, 6). But the luxuriant vine failed God's expectations. Just as the Lord multiplied the fruit in the land, so the Israelites multiplied their altars and sacred pillars. In this way they had perverted God's blessings, and He would have to withdraw them from His unfaithful people.

Hosea also warned that the calf idol from Bethel, together with the king from Samaria, would find themselves taken by Assyria, thus leaving the people without hope or purpose. The Bible clearly teaches that an idol has no value beyond that of its materials. Not being able to offer help during the invasion, the idol from Bethel epitomizes Israel's shift from glory to shame. Thorns and thistles, which symbolize the curse of the ground (Gen. 3:18), will cover the idolatrous altar. The foreign nations will be the grape harvesters used by God to strip the luxuriant vine of everything in which it prides itself.

The prophet compares Israel to a stubborn heifer in contrast to a trained and useful one (Hosea 4:16). In Bible times a yoke was an instrument of service. Farmers disciplined young animals by working them first on the threshing floor (Jer. 50:11). Yoked together, they would simply tread out the grain with their feet. At the next stage, they pulled a threshing sledge over it (2 Sam. 24:22). Such work prepared them for the more demanding task of plowing a furrow in a field (1 Kings 19:19; Jer. 4:3). God had a similar plan in training Israel. He would put a yoke on Ephraim's neck to make him work hard in plowing and breaking up the soil, just as a beast of burden participates in various agricultural tasks.

The Lord plans to work together with His people in a mutual relationship to bring blessings back to the land: "Sow righteousness for yourselves, reap the fruit of unfailing love, and break up your unplowed ground; for it is time to seek the Lord, until he comes and showers his righteousness on you" (Hosea 10:12). The admonition to sow righteousness concerns relationships among people, while searching for the Lord focuses on the relationship between people and God.

In the beginning of their history as a nation the Lord had disciplined Israel (verse 11) and He still had hopes for them (verse 12). But not long afterward, they failed to meet those expectations (verse 13). Since the nation has refused to appreciate God's goodness, its lot will become much harder. The entire process, from plowing to reaping, has turned sour because of the problem with the quality of the seed sown in the ground. In spite of this sad reality Hosea declares that the present is a ripe time to seek the Lord so that He could provide for the needs of His people. When God yokes Israel to work in open fields, righteousness and kindness will grow.

Jesus applies to His followers the metaphor of Israel as God's vine cultivated and protected to bear good fruit in passages such as John 15. Those who are faithful depend on Him in the same way in which the branches do the vine. But the people of Hosea's time failed to realize that without God they could accomplish nothing. In His time, Jesus denounced unfaithful leaders by saying that the kingdom of God would be taken from them and given to a nation that would bring good fruit (Matt. 21:43). Christ also offered comfort to all who felt tired and burdened: "Come to me, all you who are weary and burdened, and I will give you rest. Take my yoke upon you and learn from me, for I am gentle and humble in heart, and you will find rest for your souls. For my yoke is easy and my burden is light" (Matt. 11:28-30).

God Will Not Give Up
Hosea's most effective metaphors to describe God's love come from

the personal and intimate language of the family setting. Chapter 11 portrays God as the caring parent and Israel as the rebellious son. The picture of a child conveys helplessness and inability to bear the responsibilities of adulthood. The ancient Near East commonly used the paternal metaphor to express the relation between ruler and ruled, sovereign and subject. The text contrasts the tender, loving actions of the parent with those of the rebellious and ungrateful son. The prophet depicts the Lord as a parent grieving over His rebellious child who has turned away in spite of the love and care poured out on him. As the firstborn son, Israel is variously called Ephraim and *Ammi* "my people."

God had called His son out of Egypt and then established a special covenant relationship with him. Later on, however, Israel walked away from the divine Parent. The call of the idols proved stronger than God's, and this led to Israel's capitulation to the worship of Baal. Yet God still remembers how He taught Ephraim to walk, holding him by his arms to steady him in his first steps. The other nurturing gestures included carrying, holding, healing, and feeding. The more God did this for His son, the more the child abandoned His parent while worshipping idols, and refusing to repent.[16]

The threat of destruction is comparable with the fate of the cities of the plain (Gen. 14:2, 8; 19:24-29), whose names became proverbial for utter and irrevocable destruction. With the prospect of such a harsh punishment, God appears to struggle to control His deep feelings, since it arouses all His compassion. As a result, He changes the penalty from the threat of a total and swift destruction to a period of captivity. God's deep love for Israel prevents Him from abandoning His son. It triumphs in the struggle as He decides that the punishment will be temporary. "That is the first destruction, which in this passage seems inevitable. God is promising a process of renewal and salvation that begins *after* that. Those who survive the catastrophe need not fear a coming calamity."[17] After a period of captivity some of the people will return home. God will roar like a lion, and they will return like birds in the spring.

Every generation knows the struggle of parent-child relations. The parental love of a child is a profound bond that crosses all times and places. The rebellious child will for sure receive punishment, but the severity of discipline does not correspond to the extent of disobedience. God's ultimate plan for the straying child is reconciliation and healing. His love overtakes His anger. "Covenant love overrode covenant law, and mercy beyond judgment was promised. In each offer of hope, [Hosea's language] turns intensely personal and familial: God is a disciplining but forgiving Husband in 2:14-23 and 3:1-5; he is a healing and reconciling Lover in 14:1-8; he is an authoritative yet compassionately forbearing Parent in 11:1-11."[18] Just as loving parents will not give up on their children, so God will not give up on His people.

Hosea 11 is one of the Bible's greatest passages on God's love, forgiveness, and acceptance. No matter how bitterly we disappoint God and no matter how far we have strayed from Him, He still loves us. Once this sinks deep into the heart, it changes the sinner. The Lord, while He feels the human emotions of hurt and anger, chooses to rise above them to show love and compassion. His love is not weak or just sentimental, but it is rather dependable and strong. It promises to bring healing to the repentant sinner.

Israel's Many Sins

Hosea's twelfth chapter begins with the statement that Ephraim pursues and feeds on the east wind that blows from the desert, bringing no rain (Hosea 13:15). Pursuing it symbolizes Israel's futile foreign policy that vacillated between the two superpowers of the time, Egypt and Assyria. The prophet calls on the people to learn a lesson from the history of their nation. Jacob, their forefather, wrestled with his brother Esau and later with God Himself. He also asked for God's favor, received a blessing, and in the end was transformed.

The passage recalls both Jacob's failures and his readiness to return to God. The children of Israel did not follow the example set by the father of their nation long before them. So Hosea summons his listeners to be the true children of Jacob, or Israel, and return to the Lord in humility and repentance. After all, the whole nation had received its name from Jacob's new name, Israel, the title that demonstrates the character transformation of the patriarch after his encounter with the divine. The narrative from Genesis testifies that in the end he not only survived the encounter with God, but also prevailed. Thus he became a model of true repentance to all who face their own weaknesses and who hope for something better. Hosea's use of the full title "the Lord God of hosts" (NRSV) turns the focus away from idols toward the glory of Israel's God who is also the God of the whole world. This unique divine name reminds Israel of its total and expectant dependence on the Lord.

As Jacob learned not to trust in his wealth, so his descendants needed to learn the same lesson (Hosea 12:7-9). Their destiny was secure in the hands of the One who is truly in charge. His judgment will lead Israel to an abandonment of prosperity and to a return to an austere tent-dwelling in the wilderness. During the replay of the past idyllic time, the relationship between God and Israel will be in perfect covenantal harmony.

God could not remain silent in the face of Ephraim's selfish greed and foolish ambitions. His servants the prophets played a key role in the founding and preservation of the nation. Their ministry sharply contrasted with the worthless and empty worship of pagan idols at the popular shrines.

Hosea declares that the Lord is ready to act again through a prophet—perhaps someone in the likeness of Jacob, Moses (Num. 12:7; Deut. 34:10), or even Elijah, who began the larger prophetic movement in Israel. This ideal prophet will point to God as the living Lord. If Israel refuses to return to Him, God will deliver the nation over to destruction. The prophets, who are His agents of revelation, can also become His agents of punishment.[19] Hosea calls on his hearers to "return to your God, hold fast to love and justice, and wait continually for your God" (Hosea 12:6, NRSV). As Jacob traveled to a foreign land to find a wife, so God traveled to Egypt to rescue His people from slavery through His servant Moses. In a similar way, Hosea here presents the Lord's journey to the lands of exile with the purpose of rescuing His people from captivity.

Hosea 13 presents a series of short judgment speeches that restate the book's major themes. The first of them expresses the tragic reversal of Ephraim's prestige and power. Being Joseph's son, Ephraim once held prominence among the tribes of Israel. The cause of its tragic fall from glory to shame is the worship of the golden idols (1 Kings 12:16, 26-30). Their presence threatened to misrepresent God and destroy the right way to worship. The biblical prophets regarded the idols' existence as "*the* sin" in Israel. People kissed the images as part of the worship ritual (1 Kings 19:18). But idols could never be substitutes for God, because they were only the work of skilled human hands. God's coming judgment will fit the crime. Those who practice worthless worship will become themselves worthless. Like morning clouds, dew, chaff, or smoke, they will vanish quickly and be reduced to nothing.

Since the time of the exodus from Egypt and the wilderness period, God had revealed Himself under His personal name Yahweh, which means "HE IS."[20] This name points to the essence of life which is in God and to His eternal nature. He had provided for the needs of the people, but when they were satisfied, they forgot Him. Hosea compares the ensuing threat of judgment to attacks by ferocious beasts such as lion, leopard, and bear. Like a female bear, bereaved of her cubs, God threatens to rip the chest open and snatch the proud heart that led to forgetfulness. Once Israel's Redeemer executes the punishment, who else can provide help on which to fall back? Neither king nor princes, but God is the only giver and taker of life.

Ephraim's unpredictable behavior frustrates the Lord. At the time of his birth, the child fails to present himself. This type of stubbornness endangers the lives of both mother and infant. The child runs the risk of making the mother's womb his "eternal tomb."[21] He is an unwise son whose folly prevents him from making the decision to trust God and return to the one who has power to ransom from death and destruction. Hosea called on his audience to place their complete trust in God's inexhaustible power before a scorching wind from the east or a devouring sword puts an end to everything. The New Testament teaches that through Christ's death and resurrection we have ransom and redemption from sin and eternal death. Only Jesus can break the power of death and shatter the strength of its realm. God makes the promise: "I AM your plague, O Death!" (see 1 Cor. 15:55-57).

The Blessings of Obedience

The last chapter of Hosea is a fitting climax to the message presented in the whole book. It describes Israel's transformation and restoration that resembles a colorful rainbow after the storm. The chapter first presents yet another call to return to God, followed by the Lord's positive response to His people's repentance. The end of the chapter invites the reader to persist in a godly lifestyle. It reaffirms the promise that God's salvation will have the last word.

Hosea condenses the powerful call to repentance and hope in the words "Return, Israel, to the Lord your God!" (Hosea 14:1). Jewish communities customarily read the passage on the Sabbath preceding the Day of Atonement. When the nation returns, the Lord will also take them back to Himself. But it must begin with a categorical rejection of the sins that have caused Israel's separation from God. The nation will have to stop trusting in Assyria, or in its own military force, or even its many idols. Hosea here defines idolatry as the situation in which a maker bows down to his or her creation. God will show His mercy only to those who recognize their helplessness. He promises to love them freely.

The prophet records God's response to His people's return in the form of a love song (Hosea 14:4-8). It promises that love will be bestowed and anger withdrawn. Since the divine judgment has inflicted wounds, restoration will come in the form of healing as refreshing as the dew that provides moisture to flowers and trees during the long and dry summers of Israel (Isa. 26:19). Just as the dew covers the ground night after night, so the Lord provides grace day after day. God's people will flourish as a beautiful lily, a strong cedar tree, a valuable olive tree, or a fruitful grapevine. They will become a garden full of blessing to the whole world. A number of powerful images of love describe God's renewed relationship with His people.

The book closes with a wisdom saying. The metaphor of two ways illustrates the consequences of faithfulness on the one hand and disloyalty to God on the other. Hosea urges the reader to heed the warning about judgment and rejoice in the promises of hope. In His sermon on the mount, Jesus taught that as far as the decision to follow God is concerned, there is no middle ground. Each person has to choose between the wide and narrow gates (Matt. 7:13, 14), good and bad fruit (Matt. 7:15-18), a house built upon the rock or on the sand (Matt. 7:24-27). Both Hosea's book and Christ's preaching clearly present the way back to the Lord through the path of divine healing and restoration. God's final appeal in Hosea's book is worded in a particularly positive and hopeful manner: "Ephraim, what more have I to do with idols? I will answer him and care for him. I am like a flourishing juniper; your fruitfulness comes from me" (Hosea 14:8). Like a forgiving parent or a wounded lover who longs for the renewal of a relationship, the Lord waits for a wayward child to come back to Him and be healed. Why would anyone turn down such a generous offer?

---

[1] Sean P. Kealy, *An Interpretation of the Twelve Minor Prophets of the Hebrew Bible* (Lewiston, N.Y.: Edwin Mellen Press, 2009), p. 20.

[2] The name Jezreel has a double meaning in Hebrew.

[3] Later in Jeremiah's time the people attributed their blessings to the worship of the queen of heaven. They said to Jeremiah: "At that time we had plenty of food and were well off and suffered no harm" (Jer. 44:17).

[4] Hebrew *Bemidbar*.

[5] Abraham J. Heschel, *The Prophets* (Peabody, Mass.: Prince Press, 2001), p. 51.

[6] Charles L. Aaron, Jr., *Preaching Hosea, Amos, and Micah* (St. Louis: Chalice Press, 2005), p. 26.

[7] J. Dybdahl, *Hosea-Micah*, p. 48.

[8] Heschel, p. 51.

[9] Dybdahl, p. 49.

[10] David A. Hubbard, *Hosea: An Introduction and Commentary,* Tyndale Old Testament Commentary (Downers Grove, Ill.: InterVarsity Press, 1989), p. 186.

[11] Gale A. Yee, "The Book of Hosea: Introduction, Commentary, and Reflections," *The New Interpreter's Bible* (Nashville: Abingdon Press, 1996), vol. 7, p. 236.

[12] 1 Sam. 15:22; Isa. 1:11, 14, 15; Jer. 6:19, 20; 7:21-23; Amos 5:21-24; Micah 6:6-8.

[13] Israel broke the covenant like the town of Adam (Hosea 5:7). Some scholars have suggested that Hosea is playing here on the name Adam, saying that Israel broke God's covenant *ke'adam,* "like it was dirt" (Hosea 6:7).

[14] Yee, p. 254.

[15] Hubbard, p. 162.

[16] Israelite society expected the parents of a rebellious son to present him before the elders of the city. If proved guilty, he was sentenced to death and stoned by the community (Deut. 21:18-21). Adultery required the same type of drastic punishment (Deut. 22:22-24).

[17] Dybdahl, p. 70.

[18] Hubbard, p. 186.

[19] Yee, p. 286.

[20] When God pronounces His name as He does here, He says that He is the great I AM (Hosea 13:7; cf. Ex. 3:14, 15; John 8:58).

[21] Yee, p. 291.

Chapter 2

Messages From the Book of Joel

In January 2010 a devastating earthquake claimed more than 200,000 human lives while also causing great devastation and suffering in the small country of Haiti. Volunteer humanitarian responses from the world community provided all sorts of aid and support for the suffering population. An Adventist businesswoman, who came originally from Haiti but is now living in the United States, received an invitation to speak in Haiti's capital during the ceremony that marked the one-month anniversary of the terrible tragedy. According to an article from *Time,* the local Haitians consider the woman, whom they like to call "*Soeur* Junon" (Sister Junon), to be "a messenger from God." In her moving speech she called on the whole community to fast for three days as an offering of repentance. Also assuring the people that God has a plan for Haiti, she challenged them to gather courage and rebuild their nation.

When in Joel's time a locust plague such as Judah's citizens had never seen swept across the land, the prophet called the nation to repentance. In the midst of this agricultural disaster God's Spirit moved Joel to proclaim a time of fasting and confession of sin. He served as a mediator between the suffering nation and their God. The locust plague was one of the covenant curses described by Moses (Deut. 28:38, 42). Moreover, one of the 10 plagues that struck the land of Egypt before Israel's exodus was devastation by the locusts (Ex. 10:1-6). After announcing the Lord's involvement in the locust plague that struck the sinful nation, Joel instructs the people to "declare a holy fast; call a sacred assembly" (Joel 1:14). A prayer of repentance offered by the community would lead to healing both the people and the land.

The name Joel means "the Lord is God." It is appropriate to the overall theme of the book in declaring that only God is completely holy and just, and that He is sovereign on earth. The history of His people, as well as that of the nations, is secure in His hands. A short book of 73 verses, Joel occupies the second place in the Book of the Twelve Prophets. Scripture does not indicate the time of his ministry. Different scholars place it from the ninth century B.C. to the fourth century B.C. The traditional dating is preexilic, more precisely, the period between Hosea and Amos. "The book brings with it a message that was a matter of life or death for Judah, but Joel also deliberately directs that message to every age (cf. 1:3), and thus this prophetic literature is never out of date."[1]

In describing the devastating nature of judgment, Joel goes beyond the locust plague. The list of judgments consists of drought, fire, and military invasion. The prophet described the plague in his days as a foreshadow of the glorious appearance of "the day of the Lord" (Joel 1:15; 2:1, 11, 31) and warned that an even more terrible day of judgment was coming for which the people needed to prepare themselves. Thus the book presents the concept of two "days of the Lord," one immediate and the other future. As we consider the agricultural disaster and the events foretold on the day of the Lord, we might wonder, *Is the Lord merciful or hostile to His creation?* Joel 2:14 offers an answer through a very tentative question: "Who knows?" That is to say, we should never take God's abundant grace for granted.

The overall teaching of Joel's book is that God's goodness and reliability are evident particularly in times of crisis. The book's message is a monument to a confident hope that He does not forget those who pray for help. The New Testament gives passages from Joel prominent places in the interpretation of key events such as the outpouring of God's Spirit on the day of Pentecost (Joel 2:28-32).[2] The sermon Peter delivered on that occasion is full of words and phrases from Joel (Acts 2:17).

Tell the Children

The first verse in Joel introduces the book and characterizes it as a prophetic message from the Lord. "The word comes from outside of the prophet, not from his own inner musings (cf. Jer. 16:15; Eze. 3:1-3)."[3] It was common for the prophets to begin their proclamation by using the command "Hear!" (Joel 1:2). When employed in the Bible, the word included the concepts of both listening and remembering. The introduction to the book is short because the message is very urgent. Getting to the message quickly is the prophet's aim.[4] Joel's prophecy begins with a call to lamentation and repentance in the face of tragedy coming in response to people's sins. It has been rightly observed that biblical "prophets did not interpret the Word of God on the basis of the events they witnessed. Rather, they interpreted the events on the basis of the word revealed to them from God.

. . . For us that means that our times do not interpret the Bible. Rather, the Bible interprets our times."[5]

The locust plague is unusually severe. Earlier generations had not witnessed such a terrible calamity, and later generations would remember it well (Joel 1:3). Thus the everlasting truth and relevance gets passed down from one generation to the next (cf. Ex. 12:26, 27; Deut. 4:9; Ps. 78:4). Joel portrays the locusts as a mighty army that laid the land bare. The phrase "without number" found in Joel 1:6 also describes the locust plague that struck Egypt: "He spoke, and the locusts came, grasshoppers without number" (Ps. 105:34). The plague strikes every area of life. With every part of society affected, it became a national disaster of immense proportions. The prophet seeks to emphasize the overwhelming nature of the catastrophe. The ecological destruction could cripple the nation's economy for years to come. In addition to the loss of food, shade, and wood supply, the threat of topsoil erosion existed. Some fruit trees in Palestine take 20 years of growth before they become productive. In fact, agricultural devastation and deforestation were typical tactics of invading armies seeking to punish those they conquered by making any prospect of a short-term recovery impossible.

The prophet summons people to humble themselves before the Lord and to call on His name, because He is the only one who can save them. The text raises a number of questions to which no final answers have been given. One such question has to do with the plague of locusts. Is Joel describing a locust plague through images of a military attack, or is he depicting a military attack through word pictures of a locust plague? Scholars also debate whether the four terms applied to the locusts describe four different types of locusts or four different stages in the insect's life (Joel 1:4). Since emphasis by repetition (parallelism) is common in Hebrew, the four words for locusts convey the intensity of the destruction brought about by successive waves of insect attacks. In fact, the use of four different terms suggests a concept of completeness. An ancient Jewish commentator suggested that the four kinds of locusts refer to four nations that will rule over Israel, namely Babylon, Persia, Greece, and Rome (cf. Dan. 2; 7). Today, however, most interpreters believe that the plague was literal.

The Bible often associates vines and fig trees (Joel 1:7) with peace and prosperity (1 Kings 4:25; Micah 4:4; Zech. 3:10). Since wine will no longer be available, even normally intoxicated people begin to realize in their forced sobriety that judgment has fallen on them. The drunkards would be the first to suffer because their happiness depended on the fruit of the vine. The prophet personifies Jerusalem as a young woman told to mourn as a virgin would over the death of her betrothed. Mourning also occurs in the Temple which now lacks regular grain and drink offerings. Verse 10 introduces a drought that followed the locust plague. This calamity too was one of the covenant blessings that could turn into a curse because of disobedience (cf. Lev. 26:3-5; 9, 10; Deut. 28:1-12). Grain and fresh and dried fruit have now all withered. Normally joyful harvest time has now turned into a period of sorrow.

Joel bids the priests who mediate between God and the people to proclaim a public fast of lamentation, one that usually lasted for a day. Sackcloth was a costume of mourning and repentance (Jonah 3:5, 6). The entire population, young and old, men, women, and children, need to attend a public assembly to pray and confess their sins before God. They are to heed the Lord's urgent call to repentance and thus restore their broken relationship with Him, but with no guarantee that doing so will deliver them from the consequences of their sins. The prophet also proclaimed that the present disaster is only a foretaste of the coming day of the Lord. That day is a time when the Lord acts by altering dramatically the regular course of events.

The chapter closes by showing the effects of the calamity on the world of nature. The flaming heat of the sun has scorched the land. The cattle, deprived of water and pasture, wander in the barren fields and moan in hunger (Joel 1:18-20). The wild animals cry to God (cf. Ps. 42:1), recognizing Him as their master, and thus show the humans to whom to direct their cry of lament. If the beasts call upon the Lord's help, "how much more should his people who have been summoned to fasting and prayer."[6]

A number of biblical passages portray God as the Lord of nature. Not only has He created the world and sustains it by His power, but He also uses the natural world for divine purposes. When a natural catastrophe takes place, people need to interpret it as a call to repentance. Turning away from God will result in droughts, forest fires, storms, and floods. The Bible teaches that human sins affect and even corrupt nature (Rom. 8:22). When people forsake God, the power of death begins to reign in the natural world.

Sin constitutes turning away from a relationship with God and going after one's own desires. The Lord hates sin and cannot tolerate it. He will in the end do completely away with it. The New Testament teaches that on the judgment day all people will stand before Him to give answer to the question of how they had responded to His offer of salvation. Yet pride often keeps people from volunteering a confession or asking for forgiveness.

Both Jesus and John the Baptist began their public ministries by stating the urgency of repentance. John proclaimed: "Repent, for the kingdom of heaven has come near" (Matt. 3:2), while Jesus announced: "The time has come. . . . The kingdom of God has come near. Repent and believe the good news!" (Mark 1:15). How often today do we convene prayer meetings for the purpose of a group repentance before God?

Rending of the Heart and God's Answer

More than half of Joel's book deals with a plague of locusts. The prophet vividly depicts it in graphic detail. The locusts "overrun the fields, strip trees of foliage and bark, shave gardens, shear vineyards of produce, and clatter into houses, creating a calamity of the worst dimensions."[7] Joel 2 portrays the insects as an invading army that performs God's will. The scope of their attack is connected with the judgment on the day of the Lord. The sound of the ram's horn, or *shofar*, blown from Mount Zion, sends a warning that the invasion by an enemy is imminent and will be accompanied by other calamities (cf. Hosea 8:1). Needless to say, the inhabitants of the land find themselves gripped by fear and trembling. The swarms of locust instantly turn the abundance of verdure into desolate wilderness. In appearance and swiftness the insects resemble war horses (Joel 2:4). The noise of their wings and the crunching of their jaws are like the rumble of war chariots. They are attacking the cities of the land, and nothing seems powerful enough to stop their relentless assaults. Although some of the locusts perish, their invasion is unstoppable.

When natural disasters take place, they provoke many questions, such as "Why did God allow this to happen?" "Why have some people lived, while others have died?" Yet the best question to ask would be: "Is there a lesson here to learn?" Joel had no doubt that the locust plague could lead to a deeper insight into God's universal plan. The signs in the sky, such as the darkening of the sun, moon, and stars, indicate that the Lord is executing judgments on the earth. His voice sounds like thunder while His powerful armies execute His commands. It brings to mind the question: Who can endure the events of such a great and terrible day? (cf. Joel 2:11; Rev. 6:17).

The prophet answers that only repentant people can feel safe. Not spending much time analyzing their failings, he is far more interested in dwelling on the cure prescribed by Israel's divine Physician. So before it is too late the Lord graciously calls people to return to Him wholeheartedly, surrendering completely to His sovereign will. Hearts must be rent, not just garments, as the sign of an inward change in attitude. For His part, God is open to a change of course. He longs to forgive people's sins based on His steadfast loving-kindness (Ex. 34:6; Jonah 4:2).

The prophet's words "Who knows, He may turn and relent" (Joel 2:14) appear elsewhere in the judgment passages in Scripture, and they serve as a reminder of the Lord's absolute sovereignty over future events (cf. Amos 5:15; Jonah 3:9). We should never take divine grace for granted. Following their return to God there must be a time of anticipation among the repentant sinners. Only then will the relationship with God be repaired, the blessings restored, and the Temple offerings renewed. The "material provisions God gives his people are as much for his service as for their comfort."[8] In the end, the disaster that has struck Israel might lead the believers into a deeper relationship with their Lord.

The corporate nature of the guilt prompts the call to hold a sacred meeting to which everyone, young and old, are summoned (Joel 2:16). Facing the Temple, the priests should lead the congregation in a penitent worship service. The prayer for deliverance from calamity appeals to the dignity of God's name, asking the Lord to spare His people. God's redemptive act will prevent the neighboring nations from mocking His people and His apparent impotence. The prophet argues that the shame of the people is at the same time the shame of their God. Their loss is His loss, their defeat equals His defeat. For this reason, the Lord will be jealous for His people and the threat of judgment will shift to an offer of hope and reconciliation.

Verse 18 marks the turning point not only in chapter 2 but in the whole book since it focuses on both immediate and future restorations. God's jealousy for His land is directly linked with pity for His people. It comes in response to their repentance. The Lord's consuming zeal will focus on those He loves. Both they and their land will be the recipients of divine blessings, because both suffered during the plague. The people are assured of the ends to which the Lord will go to bring them to Himself in love and compassion. From this point on, it is no longer the locust plague but God's words of hope that dominate the book's narrative. Instead of destruction, God will send grain, wine, and oil. To ensure the lasting stability, the country needs to be rid of the threats coming from the enemy in the north (cf. Isa. 14:31; Jer. 1:13-15; Eze. 39:2). The destruction of the enemy will match that brought on the land. Rejoicing now replaces the great fear formerly experienced by the inhabitants, because the Lord has now done marvelous things. His power now revitalizes all creation.

Joel announces that the abundance of rain will bring joy and gladness to the children of Zion. The early rains in Israel fall during autumn, thus ending the dry summer season. The latter rains come in the spring months, providing moisture to ensure a rich harvest. Through threshing floors and wine vats full to overflowing God will compensate the damage that the locusts have caused. The grace that He has manifested through miraculous deliverance now calls for songs of praise. As a result, His name will be fully vindicated in and around the land of Judah. It is no longer God's people but the enemies that are put to shame. Everyone alive will acknowledge God's presence, glory, and uniqueness in the world. The Lord calls His people again *Ammi,* "my people" (cf. Joel 2:27; Hosea 2:1, 23), and His lordship is unrivaled on earth.

The last part of chapter 2 begins the description of an end-time event. The outpouring of God's blessings, after a severe punishment, ushers a new era in His relationship with His people. His Spirit, which brings power and vitality, He now pours out in abundance on all people (Joel 2:28). In ancient Israel the practice of anointing served as an external sign of endowment by the Spirit. In describing this practice one could speak of the Spirit being poured out like "precious oil" (Ps. 133:2). The Spirit is poured out on God's people just like the anointing oil flows onto the heads of those whom He elected for a special ministry. The Spirit is also a gift of power bestowed on the recipients so that they might do a particular work for the Lord (Ex. 31:2-5; Judges 6:34). Only this time the Spirit's manifestation assumes worldwide proportions. A special endowment of the Spirit fills all of God's people.

No longer limited by previous restrictions, the blessing goes to the entire nation. The only reservation noted by the prophet appears in the words "everyone who calls on the name of the Lord" and "whom the Lord calls" (Joel 2:32). The expression to "call on the name of the Lord" in the Bible means, beside exclusive worship of God, to tell others what God has done and to announce God's great offer of salvation to all who would listen and accept it, especially in the midst of a hostile environment (Gen. 12:8; Ex. 33:19; 34:5; Deut. 32:3; Ps. 105:1; Isa. 12:4; Zech. 13:9). All get to know God personally and proclaim His name. Moses' prayer recorded in Numbers 11:29 becomes a reality when all of God's people, young and old, slave and free, male and female, are filled with the prophetic Spirit. Distinctions between people become superficial and get laid aside, paving the way for the Lord to give His revelations to all through dreams and visions. The renewed heart of the faithful desires nothing else than to advance God's kingdom in the world.

Powerful signs in heaven showing God at work accompany the outpouring of the Spirit on earth. They echo the miracles that happened during the time of the Exodus and God's revelation on Mount Sinai. But this time, the powerful signs are a worldwide phenomenon. Cosmic in character, they include the darkening of the sun and the bloodstained appearance of the moon. Blood gets shed in war, and it often flows in the streets while houses burn and their smoke is visible from a long distance. Moreover, in Bible times many pagan nations worshipped heavenly bodies as their gods, something that Moses said the Israelites should never do (Deut. 4:19). In this sense, Joel's prophecy predicts that the idols of the nations will begin to fade away when the Lord comes in judgment. Joel 3:15 adds that even the starry host will lose its power and no longer give its light because the presence of the Lord's glory will outshine everything.

In the face of such awesome supernatural events, we can find refuge only in the worship and proclamation of God's holy name. The survivors who escape the widespread destruction are those who respond to the Lord's call in full obedience. At Pentecost Peter quoted this very passage (Acts 2:17-21) to explain the outpouring of the Spirit on the apostles to empower them for the great witnessing work lying ahead of them. All believers who trust in the Lord and profess His name, whether Jews or non-Jews, become recipients of God's blessings. Certain elements from the description of this great and terrible day fit the language used in the Bible to describe the second coming of Christ.

Joel's prophecy about the era of the Spirit has made significant progress toward a greater reality in the arrival and ministry of Jesus. It was Christ Himself who gave His followers the gift of the Holy Spirit to be the assurance of His presence in their midst. In the early church the Spirit manifested Himself among the members "for the common good" (1 Cor. 12:7) so that God's "church may be edified" (1 Cor. 14:5). As a result, unbelievers who come to church will be convinced that they are sinners, and their hearts will be touched so that "they will fall down and worship God" (verses 24, 25).

The Spirit is God's sign of redemption, protection, and restoration. Jesus' first coming has ushered in the day of the Lord. The only hope of surviving the judgment is to call on the Lord, which is the same as to worship God (Gen. 12:8), to acknowledge that one belongs to Him, to depend on

Him for one's life (Prov. 18:10),[9] and to share the good news with those who do not know it yet. Christ's followers receive the Holy Spirit in order that they may be His witnesses "to the ends of the earth" (Acts 1:8; 2:4).

Judgment and Salvation

Joel's big picture of the day of the Lord includes scenes of both judgment and grace. God will judge the nations on the basis of their treatment of His people in accordance with His promise to Abram and Sarai: "I will bless those who bless you, and whoever curses you I will curse" (Gen. 12:3). The condemnation and destruction of the oppressor will result in the ultimate rescue of God's people. The Lord promises to restore the fortunes of His people and bring the captives back home. The process of salvation is not complete until He has punished the enemies of His people for the crimes they have committed against the faithful. The name "Valley of Jehoshaphat" designates where the Lord judges, and it is also called the "valley of decision" (Joel 3:14). The name of the valley reminds the reader of God's great victory over a coalition of Israel's enemies during the reign of King Jehoshaphat (2 Chron. 20). The enemy had parceled out the land that belongs to God and that He regards as His heritage. "The land never belonged to Israel, but was loaned to the nation by God, and God is always understood in the [Bible] as the true owner of the land (cf. Lev. 25:23; Deut. 30:15-20; Eze. 33:23-29)."[10] The inhumane deeds done against those whom God calls *Ammi,* "My people," the Lord now punishes. Their enemies have depersonalized and treated as property or goods those who belonged to God.

The cities associated here with slave trading are Tyre, Sidon, and the five cities of the Philistines confederation (the *Pentapolis*). They committed such crimes not just against fellow human beings, but against their Creator-God. The enemy also profited during the looting of the palace and the Temple in Jerusalem. The punishment will reverse the fortunes so that the captives will be set free, while the captors' sons and daughters will become slaves and will be dispersed to distant lands in the desert. "The retribution is exact: the Hebrews, who had no love for the sea, were sold to sea peoples; the people of Phoenicia and Philistia, seasoned sea-goers, will be sold to the Sabeans, desert dwellers."[11]

The Lord summons the nations to prepare for battle (Joel 3:9, 10). People are to forge agricultural tools into instruments of war. Joel 3:10, in particular, reverses the vision of Isaiah 2 and Micah 4 in which the weapons of war are beaten into tools of peace. But in Joel even the weak ones should volunteer to be warriors. The Lord also musters His armies to meet the enemies and punish them because they have cruelly mistreated His people. The prophet further describes judgment through the metaphor of harvest. The wickedness on earth is so great that the people are ripe for judgment (cf. Isa. 63:1-6; Matt. 13:36-43; Rev. 14:14-20). Multitudes throng the valley. The Lord Himself carries out the verdict in His role as "the Judge of all the earth" (Gen. 18:25). He brings down the angelic warriors to destroy the enemy forces gathered together in the valley of decision. The names Egypt and Edom epitomize all of God's enemies as the two hostile countries often appear in prophetic oracles against foreign nations (Isa. 34; Jer. 46; Eze. 30-32).

The sky darkens, and the Lord intervenes this time through the sound of His voice that is like a lion's roar (cf. Amos 1:2). God, whose dwelling is in Zion, assures His people of His protection. In contrast with the judgment against the enemies there stands a promise of perpetual prosperity for Judah and its capital city. This is why Joel's book ends with a vision of a transformed world. The river flowing in the midst of the New Jerusalem points to the very presence of the Eternal God among a forgiven people (Joel 3:18-21). In the day of the Lord the Promised Land will flow with milk and grape juice, reversing the devastation previously caused by the locusts. A fountain of living water will issue forth from the Lord's house. God's dwelling in Zion guarantees that the enemy will never again triumph over His people. In the words of another prophet, Ezekiel, Jerusalem's new name will be *Yahweh Shammah,* "The Lord Is There" (Eze. 48:35).

Nobody can dispute the fact that evil is very real in our world. Yet God promises to deal decisively with it in His appointed time and manner. The prophetic perspective on history is grounded in faith, and it affirms that God is still in charge of our world in spite of all appearances to the contrary. This fact becomes very evident during the climatic day of the Lord. Joel's messages assure the faithful that eternal life in God's kingdom can be ours. Elsewhere, the Bible teaches that the believers' destiny is a full enjoyment of God's presence, both now and forever (Rev. 21; 22).

A century or so ago a tourist visited a famous Jewish rabbi. The man could not hide his surprise when he saw that the teacher's home was just a simple room with a few pieces of furniture and many books. "Teacher, where is your furniture?" he asked.

"And where is yours?" the teacher replied.

"But I am only a visitor here," the tourist said.

"So am I," the rabbi answered. "So am I!"

[1] Elizabeth Achtemeier, "The Book of Joel: Introduction, Commentary, and Reflections," *The New Interpreter's Bible* (Nashville: Abingdon Press, 1996), vol. 7, p. 302.

[2] S. Kealy, *An Interpretation of the Twelve Minor Prophets of the Hebrew Bible*, p. 29.

[3] Achtemeier, p. 305.

[4] J. Dybdahl, *Hosea-Micah*, p. 89.

[5] Achtemeier, p. 305.

[6] David A. Hubbard, *Joel and Amos: An Introduction and Commentary*, Tyndale Old Testament Commentary (Downers Grove, Ill.: InterVarsity Press, 1989), p. 53.

[7] Doug R. Clark and John C. Brunt, eds., *Introducing the Bible* (Lanham, Md.: University Press of America, 1997), vol. 1, p. 407.

[8] Hubbard, *Joel and Amos*, p. 59.

[9] Achtemeier, p. 328.

[10] *Ibid.*, p. 330.

[11] Hubbard, *Joel and Amos*, p. 77.

Chapter 3:

Messages From the Book of Amos

In his classic work "The Grand Inquisitor" Russian writer Dostoyevsky depicted the institution of the church in his time as having things so well under control that it did not need Christ anymore. An artificial form of godliness masked the lack of any genuine devotion to spiritual things. It had led to an absence of the transforming power of God. Yet the church leaders of the time held others accountable for what they themselves failed to do.

The book of Amos informs us that a similar situation afflicted the people of Israel centuries before the time of Christ. Those in Amos' day felt secure in their fortified cities, their well-polished religion, and their prosperity. But, moved by God's Spirit, Amos preached that God holds all people responsible for their actions, beginning with the leaders of the northern kingdom of Israel.

Scholars believe that Amos was the initial writing prophet and also that he was the first prophet who applied the message of the judgment to the whole nation of Israel rather than to individuals. He particularly denounced two sins: the abuse of power in society and the worship of foreign gods. The powerful and wealthy elite lived and behaved as if they were always right, while the less-privileged people viewed God as a ruthless aristocrat. When they worshipped, the people sought to please themselves rather than the Lord.

The home of Amos was in Tekoa, a town located about 10 miles south of Jerusalem in the southern kingdom of Judah. His original and main vocation was pastoral (a sheep raiser) and also agricultural (a planter or a trimmer of sycamore trees). It explains his use of many metaphors derived from country life. Some scholars have concluded that Amos was a wise and well-informed farmer. His prophetic ministry spanned a short period of about two years around 760 B.C. during the reigns of King Uzziah and King Jeroboam II and prior to the rise of the Assyrian king Tiglath-Pileser III.

Amos was a lay prophet without any connection to a local shrine or membership in a group of prophets sponsored by the royal palace in Samaria. His book consists of five short visions and several condensed prophetic speeches. Through them, the prophet linked pagan worship with corrupt social practices that had all prompted God's judgment. Amos' favorite topic was justice.[1] We could condense his message to the leaders of Israel and the surrounding nations in a single sentence: "You should have known better." The end of the book points toward hope beyond divine punishment. Divine promises of salvation assure the ultimate restoration of the faithful remnant.

This prophetic book abounds in a variety of rhetorical and literary forms such as judgment speeches, vision reports, biographical narratives, salvation promises, admonitions and instructions for living, hymns of praise, woes and lamentations, and repetitions and wordplays. Throughout the book poetic passages mix with conversations between the Lord and the prophet, and they combine with narratives about Amos' conflicts with the leaders who tried to oppose his ministry. As was the case with the other great prophets, Amos used "what he had acquired from the traditions of his people and their faith and then with startling artistry, under the influence of the Spirit's guidance, recombined the literary approaches into an assemblage that can only be called unique, original, and compelling."[2]

He demonstrated great courage not only in proclaiming the divine messages but also in defending his prophetic authority when challenged by certain individuals. His convictions rested on the assumption that God's words are an extension of the Lord's own person. It meant that everyone who heard them must take them seriously. Amos' message came as a big surprise to his audience because he reversed the cherished popular traditions and turned them back on his hearers. Needless to say, his words were not popular.[3] Together with the other early prophets in the Bible, he addressed a big dilemma in Israel's history: Did God's covenant with His people continue after Israel's repeated unfaithfulness had broken it? The prophet proclaimed that instead of escaping the judgment on the day of the Lord, the nation of Israel would go through it in accordance with God's covenant regulations. An earthquake confirmed Amos' announcement of the coming of this judgment (Amos 1:1; cf. Zech. 14:5).

The message of Amos' book consists of stern condemnations of the sins of both leaders and people who practiced neither justice nor righteousness. The prophet announced an end to the northern kingdom of Israel. "A nation that could not be corrected had to be rejected."[4] The same Lord of Hosts who had led Israel out of Egypt, now took on Himself the full responsibility for the coming devastation of the land and its people by the cruel forces of Assyria. The prophet compares God's coming to judge His creatures with all its terror and surprise to the roar of a lion, the king of the animal world.

Amos' personal encounter with the "divine Lion," whose roaring he had heard during his call to prophesy for God, had greatly shaped his ministry. The prophet was convinced that all the nations of the earth, including Israel, along with all nature were under the power and authority of the one Lord. He urged his hearers to translate their worship of God into everyday conduct. The early Christian believers understood Amos' book to contain words that both comfort and confront. Thus Stephen used the text from Amos 5:25-27 to affirm God's rejection of Israel's leaders who had spurned the testimony of the prophets and of Jesus Christ (Acts 7:42, 43). James, on the other hand, quoted Amos 9:11, 12 to explain God's plan of including Gentile peoples in the restored kingdom of King David (Acts 15:16, 17).

Human Accountability to God

The threat of a coming judgment is the main theme in Amos' book, and its announcement begins with the opening words about the lion-like roar of the Lord from Zion. The name Zion points to Jerusalem, united Israel's capital beginning with David. After the breakup of the united monarchy, it remained the capital of the southern nation of Judah. The city contained the Lord's Temple. The Lord's roar produces devastating effects on the leaders in Samaria, the capital city of the northern kingdom. (Amos refers to them as "shepherds," a common ancient Near Eastern term for kings.) In a similar way the prophet came from Judah and preached his message of judgment against the ruling classes in Samaria. The use of the messenger formula "thus says the Lord" lends authenticity to the prophetic message by tracing it to God as its ultimate source.

First, the prophet portrays God as the Sovereign who calls to account Israel's neighboring nations one by one. Did the Lord do this because He had some type of a covenant relationship with all these kingdoms? The answer to this question, according to Amos, is positive. Yet another way to approach this passage is to see God as the head of the family of nations disciplining His children. After all, isn't God the heavenly parent to all human beings who dwell on earth? All the nations are God's sons and daughters, although the Bible calls Israel His firstborn child (Ex. 4:22). All need to answer to the Creator-God whether or not they acknowledge Him. The acts of inhumanity done by these nations are also deeds of rebellion against the Creator and Lord of all humanity.

Several of Israel's neighboring nations dwelt in land that did not originally belong to them but that had been promised long ago to the biblical patriarchs and matriarchs. The accountability of these nations stood in proportion to the light given to them. That is why the prophet does not condemn them for sins of idolatry, but for crimes against humanity, especially in war situations. Amos' use of the figure of speech "For three sins and for four" puts in focus the last or seventh sin. Scripture commonly uses the number seven in passages about judgment (cf. Lev. 26; Dan. 3:19; 4:16). The seventh sin, according to Amos, filled the measure of wickedness and thus unleashed God's decisive response to cruelty and injustice.

Damascus (Amos 1:3) was the capital city of the land of Arameans, also known as the Syrians. They were closely related to the Israelites through Abraham and Jacob. In fact, in one place the Bible refers to Jacob as a "wandering Aramean" (Deut. 26:5), and centuries later the prophet Elijah anointed an Aramean army commander to be king in Damascus. Sadly, the Aramean rulers often practiced extreme cruelty during their raids on the northeastern parts of the land of Israel. Amos predicted fiery judgment on the fortresses in Damascus and its surroundings. The Arameans would be led as captives to the land of their origin in southeast Mesopotamia.

The Philistine tribes had migrated to the coastland north of Egypt from their original home on the Greek islands. Their five cities formed a confederacy *(pentapolis)*. Although the Philistines and the Hebrews often fought each other, King David at times found refuge in their territory, and later on his special royal guard consisted of men from the Philistine city of Gath. Like the Arameans, the Philistines had committed acts of inhumanity that included human trafficking and slave trading. Amos declared that because of this the walls of Philistine strongholds would prove helpless when God judges them (Amos 1:7).

During the time of David and Solomon the Phoenicians were close allies of Israel through a treaty of brotherhood (1 Kings 5:12). Despite this, the people of Tyre, the Phoenician main city, demonstrated extreme greed when they sold entire settlements from Israel into slavery in Edom. Because of this, both the Phoenicians and the Edomites, whose soldiers committed crimes of violence against innocent men and women, would not escape the coming judgment. Of all the neighboring nations, Edom was Israel's closest kin because their ancestor Esau was Jacob's twin brother. So the Edomites traded as slaves people who were their own "flesh and blood." Amos concluded by saying that fire would consume both capital cities, Tyre and Bozrah.

The descendants of Lot's two sons, Ammon and Moab, occupied the territory east and northeast of the Dead Sea. Through Abraham, Lot's uncle, they were related to the Israelites, but like the Edomites they had also attacked Israel and Judah. Amos denounced the Ammonite soldiers for their extreme cruelty during military confrontations against helpless women and innocent unborn children (Amos 1:13). Once the Moabites even desecrated the bones of an Edomite ruler. Because of their crimes, the king of Moab would die in the destructive fire while the people of Ammon would face captivity.

Amos now turns to the land of Judah located south of Israel. Popular traditions of the time had led the chosen people to believe that on the day of the Lord, God would judge the non-Hebrew nations while delivering His special people and exalting them. But the prophet's message contained a great surprise, because he proclaimed that on that great day God would also judge His chosen people. They too were accountable to the supreme Judge who does not play favorites.

The prophet denounced his own homeland, because its people failed to keep the instructions given to them by God through Moses (Amos 2:4). Instead they worshipped false gods and idols. Idolatry is a type of religious self-deception. The Bible describes idols as nothing or as vanity and certainly not worthy of worship. The people had broken their covenant with God, and covenant curses would be poured on the land of Judah, targeting especially its ruling elite. The instrument of judgment would be fire that would strike the land in whose center was the city of David, the man after God's own heart. Although King David never worshipped idols, his descendants did not follow his example of undivided faithfulness to God.

The primary focus of Amos' prophecy was the land of Israel to which the Lord had sent him to deliver a solemn and urgent warning. The prophetic indictment against the northern kingdom of Israel is longer than the previous ones, while the list of crimes is more detailed. The acts of rebellion that Amos cites consisted of the material and religious exploitation of fellow human beings. The nation abused its privileged status, oppressed the poor, corrupted its worship, broke God's covenant, and committed immoral acts (Amos 2:6-8). The strong in Israelite society abused their power and treated unjustly not some foreign nation but their own people.

A holy God hates greed, immorality, and injustice. Amos confronted Israel with the fact that they, together with their possessions, belonged to the Lord. He had given His people victories over those who had once inhabited the land of Canaan. Yet whenever His messengers tried to remind the people of their responsibilities, the leaders would silence them. God had no other choice but to smash His land just as a cart is crushed when overloaded by a farmer (verse 13). The Lord would use fire, war, and earthquake to discipline His people. Terror would grip the hearts of even the bravest soldiers. All the threats presented by the prophet had one purpose: to call the unfaithful people back to God before it was too late and to tell them to renounce unfaithfulness and oppression.

Speeches Against Israel

Amos' proclamation contained the tragic announcement of divine judgment because the people of Israel had abused their God-given privileges and spurned His covenant. Towns such as Samaria and Bethel, which should have been centers of blessing, had become focal points of injustice and idolatry. Amos said that the chosen people would no longer be the object of special blessings and privileges but would instead suffer punishment and destruction. Israel forgot that the covenant with God entailed not only blessings for obedience but also curses for disobedience. When centuries before Jacob's family had been enslaved in Egypt, God had provided freedom, but now the people had become slaves to idols. In the beginning of its history the nation prospered and its people multiplied, but now, steeped in sin, they would become decimated and impoverished.

The prophet proceeds to ask seven questions that go from effect to cause, following the typical Hebrew way of thinking (Amos 3:3-7). The logical premise is that there can be no result without cause. The purpose of the questions was to establish the fact that Israel's history lay in God's hands. Events in history do not take place without His involvement. "When disaster comes to a city, has not the Lord caused it?" (verse 6). No! The Lord does nothing without first telling about it to His prophets. Given access to the heavenly council, they are well informed of His plans (Jer. 23:18-22). They then warn the people about the approaching judgment.

When God had made covenant with Israel, the primary witnesses, according to Moses, were heaven and earth (Deut. 4:26; 30:19). Amos now summons foreign observers to witness the legal dispute between God and His faithless people. Even the standard of behavior of foreigners could easily show by whose fault the covenant had been broken. The coming judgment would have a purifying effect on the people, and a surviving remnant would serve as a material proof that the nation had come to its end. Just as a leg bone or a piece of an ear snatched from the jaw of a wild beast proved the loss of an animal, so would Israel's small remnant show that the Lord had judged the nation (Amos 3:12). As a sheep raiser, Amos was familiar with the requirement of a shepherd to present some pieces of an animal killed by a wild beast to refute that he had stolen it and that it had indeed been destroyed through no failure of his own.

The family of Jacob went through a spiritual renewal in and around the city of Bethel. But Amos taught that God would judge this same city when the horns of its altar—symbolizing power—would be shattered to pieces (verse 14). Another city where Jacob's sojourn had been eventful was the city of Shechem in the region of Samaria. Amos warned that invaders would level to the ground many of the luxurious houses decorated with ivory in the city of Samaria. It would be the result of the abuse of worship at the idolatrous altars at Bethel and of the wealth built on oppression by those who lived in lavish homes in Samaria.

The prophet sarcastically addresses the wealthy women as "cows of Bashan" who have grown fat and insensitive to the needs of the less privileged. Bashan was a region in Palestine proverbial for agricultural and pastoral prosperity. The Lord makes a solemn oath that He will defend the rights of the poor and needy, while enemy armies would lead the proud and greedy through the breaks in the city walls (that the invaders had made) to foreign captivity. It would be the natural outcome of the empty worship and meaningless sacrifices that Israel had presented at the local shrines.

One of the core prophetic teachings is that God's judgments are grounded in His grace, because their ultimate purpose is to bring sinners back to God. Famines, droughts, insect plagues, and military invasions should have led the people to repentance and a renewed trust in Him. That is why God takes full responsibility for such acts of discipline. Amos describes famine as "cleanness of teeth" (Amos 4:6, NRSV) during which people will wander from place to place in search of such basic provisions as grain, fruit, and vegetables. He compares the suddenness and finality of the coming destruction to the catastrophe that struck the cities of the plain, including Sodom and Gomorrah. The small surviving remnant will be like a brand plucked from the fire. They could credit their survival only to God's grace just as was the case with Lot and his daughters.

Faced with the prospect of judgment, Israel must prepare to meet God (verse 12) in a way similar to the experience at Sinai (Ex. 19:17), an event characterized by an earthquake, clouds and lightning, fire, and the sound of trumpet. Just as Moses called those who had left Egypt to consecrate themselves, so Amos is urging the present people of Israel to make the same type of preparation. A short hymn of praise composed by the prophet portrays graphically God's overwhelming glory and might. The Lord is the Creator of everything, and through worship His people celebrate His power that sustains all forms of life. No mouth can remain silent before such an awesome majesty.

"Seek the Lord!"

In anticipation of the soon death of the northern kingdom, Amos composed a short lament over Israel's end (Amos 5:2, 3). He abruptly shifts from a song about God's majesty that imparts life (at the end of chapter 4) to the lament about a tragic loss of life in chapter 5. The prophet mourns the fact that God's special daughter (described by him as a "virgin") is going to die prematurely and thus be deprived of the joys and blessings of a normal life. He depicts Israel's fate through the imagery of the decimation of its army. Facing the prospect of an inevitable judgment, a person could find refuge only in the pure worship of the Lord. Amos said that the illegitimate shrines would be of no help since they would be destroyed. Bethel, meaning "house of God," had become Beth-aven or "house of iniquity."[5]

What the Lord wants from the people is for them to practice justice and righteousness in their daily life (cf. Micah 7:9). Those who worship God must be truthful and compassionate, just as He is in His dealing with humans—the essence of the teaching that the Lord gave through Moses and the other prophets. It has been rightly said that the justice of God is more than a blindfolded woman who holds a balance in her hand. One can present it better as a gentle but strong person who stretches one arm to reach the weak while using the other arm to drive the oppressor away.[6] Yet in Amos' time the privileged elite had turned sweet justice and righteousness into bitterness. Such behavior does not go unnoticed by the Creator of all things, who is also Lord of all nature. Several short hymns scattered throughout Amos' book celebrate God's power.

In the middle of chapter 5 Amos comes back to the topic of unjust dealings in Israel. He gives a sense of an all-pervasive injustice in the society. It begins at the gate of the city where the elders were supposed to dispense justice. But, instead, they hated and despised truth and justice there (Amos 5:10). The leaders placed heavy taxes on the farmers and used them to build expensive stone houses and to plant lovely vineyards at the expense of the poor and downtrodden. Such numerous sins would lead the nation into captivity. It was a time of evil when the prudent would keep silent. The prophet, however, declared that it was still not too late to seek good and hate evil with one's whole heart. Yet one should never take the Lord's response of grace and love for granted.

The prophet contrasts the joy of the penitent with the lament of the arrogant. The lovely vineyards that burst with joy during happy times of harvest would become centers of wailing, grief, and funeral dirges. Not only will the crops fail, but a plague would target the fields and vineyards. It would be as devastating as when God passed through Egypt prior to Israel's exodus.

A prevalent concept about the day of the Lord was that during it the Lord would defeat all Israel's enemies and elevate His people above other nations. It was a hope so frequently celebrated in worship that people looked forward to the fulfillment of the divine promises about their deliverance and glorification. The problem with such teaching was that it had become rooted in absolute certainty and completely detached from everyday life. In other words, Israel viewed divine promises as blank checks given without any conditions. People thought that the practice of idolatry and social injustice, so prevalent in Israel, could never prevent or affect in any way the blessings predestined to come on the day of the Lord. Amos wanted to correct their misguided understanding. Those who clung to idols were destined to perish together with the oppressors of the weak and poor. To those who lived with such a false sense of safety, the day of the Lord would rather be "the night of the Lord," a time of darkness and not light. When they think that they may have escaped the threat of the wild beast (cf. Hosea 13:7-9) in the open field and found safety in the house, right there a poisonous snake would bite them.

A frequent and important theme in prophetic proclamations was that sacrifices or other religious ritual could never substitute for obedience to God. In other words, a multitude of gifts cannot blind His eyes. He who searches the depth of human hearts knows well the thoughts and deeds of every worshipper. The God of Israel delighted in the sweet aroma that arises from the works of justice and kindness. Worship fit for the Lord demands deeds of righteousness. Songs and prayers in the Temple need to be translated into the language and acts of everyday life in which justice and righteousness flow like a never-failing spring (Amos 5:24). A sacrifice without obedience is a meaningless shedding of blood.

When the children of Israel dwelt in the wilderness they proved to be a rebellious and ungrateful nation. They constantly murmured against God and His representatives, Moses and Aaron. On at least two occasions they followed other gods and idols (Ex. 32; Num. 25). Yet Amos said that in comparison with the present apostasy, past rebellions fade away. For this reason, God will send Israel to captivity in a land beyond Damascus where the people customarily worshipped idols and regularly performed meaningless rituals in their temples. The land beyond Damascus is Assyria, the future destiny for those who persisted in idolatry and rebellion.

Lest the reader think that only the northern kingdom of Israel was guilty of sins against God, Amos also addresses Zion (Amos 6:1). He condemns the complacency of the leaders of the southern kingdom of Judah. Like Samaria in the north, the city of Jerusalem had a false feeling of security as it hoped that evil would never come near it regardless of what it did. The citizens of both capital cities boasted of their prestige over neighboring cities. Amos sarcastically remarks that Samaria competed with the other cities in gluttony, drunkenness, and bribery. The rich lay on ivory beds and feasted on wine and meat of fattened animals while the poor lacked wheat, barley, fruit, and vegetables. Music-making accompanied luxurious daily meals. Olive oil and old wine were regularly served during such meals from expensive jars.

Since the wealthy elite craved everything that was *first* and best, they would be the *first* to go to captivity. In that distant land all their privileges would disappear. Amos saw the Lord of Israel's armies make an oath by His eternal existence in the midst of the heavenly council that judgment would soon come on the sinful nation and its proud strongholds. Even if only 10 people survived, they too would die. When a close relative entered the house to carry the corpses out to bury them, they would not dare to pronounce the Lord's name lest a greater disaster strike. The presence of God manifested in full view before the nation would be a threat to life, not a refuge from evil.

Israel's unwillingness to repent led to a verdict against all households, both great and small. The nation's stubbornness was as absurd as an attempt to race horses on rocky ground or to make oxen plow the waves of the sea. The leaders were proud of their conquest of a town named *Lo-de-var,* which means "nothingness." They also claimed to have overwhelmed another town called *Karnaim,* or "double-strength," by their own power. Amos asserts that victory comes only from the Lord of hosts who had provided His people with the gift of a special land.

Visions of Warning and Hope

The last three chapters in Amos (chapters 7-9) contain five visions that the prophet reports in the first person. During some of them Amos dialogued with God. Thus, when shown a threat of a locust plague approaching his people during the most critical period of the agricultural calendar, the prophet pleaded with God for forgiveness, because he knew that only the Lord could reverse the coming tragedy. Being compassionate, God forgave His people. The smallness of Jacob's family, whose existence a famine had long ago threatened (Gen. 40-47), worked to the nation's advantage.

Amos reacted in the same way when he saw a fire coming on the land, one so powerful that it devoured the water of the great deep. Once again the Lord relented after Amos pleaded, and he witnessed still another act of divine mercy. Biblical prophets were, in the first place, persons of prayer. Abraham (Gen. 18; 20), Moses (Ex. 32), and Daniel (Dan. 9) all interceded with God for the sake of others.

In his third vision the prophet sees the Lord as the Master Builder holding in His hand a plumb line, symbolizing another instrument of judgment. The vision compares Israel to a wall that needs to be checked for uprightness. The judgment on the nation was inevitable, so the prophet no longer pleads for forgiveness. Illegitimate shrines built in the towns would collapse when God came to visit them.

Inserted between visions three and four is the story of Amos' encounter with Amaziah, the priest at Bethel (Amos 7:10-17). This man considered the prophet's message to be a direct threat to his position as well as the rest of Israel's leaders, including the ruler in Samaria. Amaziah described Amos' attack on the shrine at Bethel as an act of conspiracy against the king. He said that the earth could no longer bear Amos' words, which, like a great flood, threatened a total destruction of the land. Yet Amaziah said nothing about the sins that were the very reason that God would send them into exile.[7] Referring to Amos as a "seer" who was not paid by the king of

Samaria, the priest ordered the prophet to return to his own country and minister there.

In his answer to Amaziah, Amos showed that he could not be intimidated. He was not a professional but a lay prophet—thus not "a prophet for hire." As such, his livelihood did not depend on any human establishment nor on the popularity of what he proclaimed. Rather, he was accountable to God who had elected him to speak for Him. Amos' call to ministry was the first and foremost sign that he was a true prophet. The Lord had told him to go to preach against the sins of the northern kingdom of Israel. As for his original profession, he was a breeder of livestock (cf. 2 Kings 3:4) and trimmer of sycamore trees.[8] Amos' ministry was not the result of his own decision, but it came from the Lord's surprise initiative. He had heard the roar of the great Lion of Judah and could not refuse to speak up. His classic answer to Amaziah has inspired countless readers of the Bible to treat God's ministers with respect.

Whereas Amos gives the account of his encounter with Amaziah in narrative prose, the judgment pronounced against the opportunist priest appears in poetry. Amos' rebuke of the priest reminds the reader of the Bible of those pronounced by great prophets such as Nathan (2 Sam. 12), Elijah (1 Kings 21), Micaiah (1 Kings 22), and Daniel (Dan. 5). God sentences Amaziah to die captive in a foreign land, his children slain, and his wife's only financial support to sell her body by working as a prostitute. As for the nation of Israel, it would go into exile. It was a case of like priest, like people (cf. Hosea 4:9). The futures of Amaziah and Israel "were inextricably entwined. The fate of the one would be the fate of the other."[9]

During Amos' fourth vision, God showed him a basket of ripe summer fruit and told him that the sinful nation of Israel was ripe for punishment that would bring its existence to an end (Amos 8:1, 2). The time for repentance had run out and mercy was no longer available. Joyful songs would turn to laments, silence would replace the sound of celebration. An earthquake, a darkening of the sun, a drought, and a lack of God's Word would accompany the Lord's withdrawal from His people. Amos pointed to God's justice and moral reasons for judgment. People tried to substitute worship for mercy and justice. Some were guilty of using dishonest weights and measures, others of trampling the poor or selling the destitute into slavery at minimal price. The Lord swore to put an end to it. When He intervened, the land would be shaken by an earthquake and would oscillate just as the water rises and sinks in the Nile. The noonday sun would darken, and there would be a lament as loud as a widow's cry for her own son.

Cosmic signs will point to the end of earth's history. The prophetic word would be scarce in those days because of a worldwide spiritual famine during which people will roam from place to place in search of God's life-giving words—but they will not find them (Amos 8:11, 12). For too long the people had rejected the messages sent by their God, so that He has now withdrawn completely. But physical hunger and thirst will also be part of divine judgment. God's heart will hurt as He sees beautiful young people starving to death. Calling a pagan deity for help will make no difference, nor will the golden calves worshipped in Dan and Bethel save the doomed nation. When the idols perish, so will those who worship them. Such is the fate of those who pray to dead idols. People become what they worship.[10]

The fifth vision portrays a total destruction on all idolaters in Israel (Amos 9:1). Whereas the neighboring nations did not receive a rebuke for their idol worship, the prophet does pronounce a complete ban on idol worshippers among God's covenant people. Amos saw the Lord[11] as the chief commander who issues orders and takes personal responsibility for the death of the rebellious. The judgment begins with the sanctuary that collapses as the Lord powerfully manifests Himself. The wicked who survive the earthquake will surely die in exile. The same Lord who took His people out of slavery will now lead the idolatrous nation into captivity.

Amos 9 is one of the clearest biblical passages about the sinner's inability to escape divine justice. While it is possible to manipulate and deceive human beings and establishments, the same is not the case with the One who knows everything. The prophet presents a series of opposite terms placed together to express the totality (merism) of God's presence in all creation. In other words, there exists no place where one can hide from God, whether in the sky above or in the world of the dead below. Neither the top of Mount Carmel, the highest place in the northern kingdom, nor the bottom of the sea, are beyond His reach. The serpent at the bottom of the deepest sea was ready to obey God's orders and punish the one who loves evil.

The Lord's amazing presence in the entire universe moves the prophet to burst again into poetry. A short poem celebrates God's cosmic power and authority over the armies of heaven. The hymn of praise begins and ends with a mention of the Lord's name. He is the God who not only provided an exodus for Israel but did similar acts of grace in behalf of other people, such as the Ethiopians and even the bitter enemies of Israel, the Philistines and Arameans (Syrians). They were God's children in addition to God's firstborn child. But Israel's privileged status could not be an excuse for irresponsible behavior. The sinful kingdom needed to go through judgment. Just as the farmer winnows the grain from the husk, so God would separate the penitent from the rebellious and thus spare them from destruction.

More than two millennia after Amos' ministry, Dominican Savonarola in Italy preached a series of sermons from Amos' book against the sins of prelates and friars that led to his condemnation and execution.[12] Today, the preaching of Amos is "an invitation to look at the world around us and see the crimes and tragedies which have been perpetrated."[13] It is true that "our standing before God depends, not upon the amount of light we have received, but upon the use we make of what we have."[14]

Yet the book of Amos concludes with a message of hope and restoration. The transition from the last vision of destruction to the promises of salvation is so sudden and surprising that some scholars have wondered if Amos really authored the closing words of the book that bears his name.[15] Was he not a consistent prophet of doom? But this text is not the only passage in Amos that opens a door to hope through repentance. Why would he entreat the people to seek their Lord if the door of salvation had been shut? Did God not reveal Himself as someone full of mercy and grace?

In the future God will restore the fortunes of His people, and He will once again rejoice in providing them with blessings. Amos casts the description of the new order of things in the language of the past. The kingship of David, Israel's model king, would again provide safety and prosperity to the nation. The people would enjoy an abundant yet simple life, just as their ancestors did in the wilderness when the Lord dwelt with His people in tents. The authority of His rulership would spread over all humanity, embracing the nations against whom Amos had before pronounced judgment. All will be able to taste and see that the Lord is good and willing to forgive, even the proud and cruel Edomites.

The hyperbolic portrayal of material property that would characterize God's reign on earth is particularly moving. In the new order of things nature will be incredibly fruitful, and the people will be secure in their land. The produce will be so abundant that the harvesting will continue through the time for planting new seeds (Amos 9:13). So plowman and reaper will work together and no longer be separated by a period of five to six months during which the seed grows and fruit ripens. Rivers of sweet and fresh grape juice will flow down the hills and mountains. When the Lord gives blessings to His people, the abundance of food and drink and His generosity will know no limits. He will address His people again as "My People." But the benefits of the messianic era will extend to the nations. God will transform all creation so as to richly bless the world to the full and permanent enjoyment of the redeemed. They will dwell in safety, and He will be their God forever. It is what the Lord had intended to do from the beginning of His covenant of love with the human race.

_____

[1] J. Dybdahl, *Hosea-Micah,* p. 108.

[2] D. Hubbard, *Joel and Amos,* p. 107.

[3] Aaron, *Preaching Hosea, Amos, and Micah,* p. 54.

[4] Hubbard, *Joel and Amos*, p. 108.

[5] Amos shows that he is an expert with wordplays when he coins a saying based on similarity of sounds (assonance): *ki gilgal galo' yigle,'* which means "for Gilgal will surely go into exile."

[6] Edmond Jacob, *Theology of the Old Testament* (New York: Harper and Row, 1958), p. 99.

[7] Dybdahl, p. 133.

[8] Donald E. Gowan, "The Book of Amos: Introduction, Commentary, and Reflections," *The New Interpreter's Bible* (Nashville: Abingdon Press, 1996), vol. 7, p. 340.

[9] Hubbard, *Joel and Amos*, p. 218.

[10] See G. K. Beale, *We Become What We Worship: A Biblical Theology of Idolatry* (Downers Grove, Ill.: InterVarsity Press, 2008).

[11] The Hebrew text has "Adonai" rather than "Yahweh."

[12] S. Kealy, *An Interpretation of the Twelve Minor Prophets of the Hebrew Bible,* pp. 41, 42.

[13] *Ibid.,* p. 45.

[14] Ellen G. White, *The Desire of Ages*, p. 239.

[15] A strong defense of Amos' authorship of this passage appears in Shalom M. Paul, *Amos*, Hermeneia (Philadelphia: Fortress Press, 1991).

Chapter 4

Messages From the Book of Obadiah

Twin sisters named Esther and Pauline were born only 17 minutes apart. Throughout their childhood they dressed the same way, took the same classes in school, and shared their personal items. Later in life, after the two sisters had gotten married, the family battle that erupted between them lasted for eight long years. Fortunately, they found a way to resolve their issues, and became partially reconciled in the end. It appears that nobody can fight as hard as siblings can. The book of Genesis tells the story of twin brothers named Esau (or Edom) and Jacob (or Israel) whose early life was full of sibling rivalry. Later, the two put their differences aside (Gen. 33).

The land of Edom was situated southeast of the Dead Sea and was also known as Seir (Gen. 32:3; 36:20, 21). In Old Testament times the Edomites, who were the descendants of Esau, lived there. Obadiah's book uses the names Esau and Edom interchangeably. Moses gave the following command to the children of Israel regarding the descendants of Esau: "Do not despise an Edomite, for the Edomites are related to you" (Deut. 23:7). Despite that, biblical records indicate a long-lasting hostility between the descendants of the two brothers. When the Israelites prepared to enter the land of Canaan, the king of Edom refused to give them permission to pass through his territory (Num. 20:14-21). Also, throughout the period of monarchy starting with Saul, Israel's first king (1 Sam. 14:47), down to Judah's king Ahaz (2 Chron. 28:17), constant warfare raged between Israel and Edom.

According to Lamentations 4:21, 22 the Edomites rejoiced at Jerusalem's destruction. Moreover, they captured the refugees from Judah and handed them over to the enemy (Amos 1:11, 12). They may have even taken a part in the sacking of Jerusalem. Thus their attitude during the time of Judah's misfortune brought curses upon their heads (Ps. 137:7). The Edomites were wrong in taking advantage of their kin's misfortune. Traditionally, they were famous for their wisdom (Jer. 49:7), but because of lack of compassion their wisdom turned to folly. Later a people called the Nabateans "invaded the Edomite mountain acropolis of Sela, where they carved their wonderful capital, the rose city of Petra, and Edom disappeared from history."[1]

Obadiah is the shortest prophetic book, consisting of only 21 verses. The Babylonian Talmud identifies Obadiah as the servant of King Ahab (1 Kings 18:3-16) who risked his life to protect God's prophets. Since the only time reference alluded to in the text of Obadiah is the fall of Jerusalem (verses 10-14), it is better to conclude that the prophet lived in a later time and delivered his message of judgment on Edom shortly after the destruction of the Jerusalem Temple in the year 587 B.C. The book announces both a local (verses 1-14) and a universal judgment (verses 15-21). The prophecy has many similarities with Jeremiah's oracle about Edom's fall (Jer. 49:7-22).

The prophet presents the judgment on Edom as retributive, that is to say, "measure for measure," making the punishment fit the crime. Obadiah declares that since Edom forgot his brother, he himself will be forgotten by his friends (verse 7). During the day of the Lord judgment will fall on Edom and all the other enemies, but those of God's people who trust in His justice will have hope. The Lord will be the judge of all nations, and deliverance will come from Zion (verse 21). Toward the end of Obadiah's book, Edom stands for all non-Hebrew nations, and the prophet contrasts Mount Zion with Mount Seir. The roles of the two mountains are, in the end, reversed. God will establish His kingly rule in all the earth while Edom's pride will come to an end.

Edom's Pride, Arrogance, and Downfall

The opening words in Obadiah describe the book as "vision," or better as "prophetic revelation," because it came to the prophet as an audition rather than a vision. The Aramaic translation, known as the Targum, describes the book as "the prophecy of Obadiah." The name "Obadiah" was common in Bible times and means "the Lord's servant, or worshipper." The short version of the name was Obed, reminding one of the name of King David's grandfather (Ruth 4:21, 22; Matt. 1:5). Scripture often refers to prophets as "servants of the Lord." As it is the case with Malachi, Obadiah is a writing prophet about whom we know only the name. The text does not even inform us about his father or the precise time he ministered.

The prophet served as the human intermediary communicating divine revelations originating from Israel's covenant God. The Lord tells Obadiah that enemy nations would soon judge Edom's pride. God, who presides over the heavenly council, here announces an impending verdict on the people of Edom. To confirm the certainty of the message, an unnamed envoy delivered it to that country. Obadiah proclaimed that Edom's fall was a part of the plan of the Lord who was sovereign in the history of the world, and that He had revealed it to humanity. The original Hebrew expresses the verdict on Edom through the use of the verbal past tense ("prophetic perfect") to enhance its certainty and to give the impression that the announced actions have already been accomplished. God's word is as good as done—that is how surely it will come to pass.

Edom's impenetrable location contributed to its great pride and arrogance (verses 2-4). The prophet compares its ambition to the soaring of an eagle. It sought to go higher than tall rocks and lofty sky, or even the stars in the heavens. Edom's capital city of Sela was a fortress in a rocky and inaccessible location. But the Lord warns that He would bring Edom down no matter how great its pride, because, as biblical wisdom books teach, pride usually goes before the fall (Prov. 16:18). Pride, arrogance, and hate make people think that they are stronger than they actually are. Moreover, pride and hate blind those infected with it, preventing them from seeing their vulnerability. Two biblical texts outside of Obadiah record Edom's boastful words shouted during Jerusalem's siege: "These two nations and countries will be ours and we will take possession of them" (Eze. 35:10). "Tear it down, . . . tear it down to its foundations!" (Ps. 137:7).

The second reason for Edom's pride was its great number of trusted allies (verses 5-7). But during the most critical time their allies and friends would prove disloyal and even treacherous. "In ancient times, alliances or covenants between individuals or peoples were considered sacred; to break a covenant was abominable; moreover, the covenant breaker was severely penalized (see Ps. 55:20; Amos 1:9)."[2] The exclamatory word "how"[3] (verse 5) begins a lament over Edom's wretched state. The prophet can see how robbers and thieves have ransacked the land. Edom's wisdom and understanding that used to enjoy international reputation will vanish along with its allies. Finally, Edom's army is annihilated. Struck by terror, even the bravest soldiers perish. So, in spite of its "high" location, Edom would be conquered and pillaged while its allies would prove treacherous. As a result, the nation faces a complete and final destruction with no remnant in sight.

The prophetic message of Edom's judgment stems from their attitude, first passive and then aggressive, regarding Judah's misfortune. In verses

10-15 the prophet lists the most important reasons for the nation's severe punishment. The foremost is Edom's violence against Israel both physical and moral. When the Babylonians destroyed Jerusalem, the Edomites offered no help to their "brothers." Instead they sided with the enemy and expressed their feelings through uncharitable behavior. First, its people laughed at Israel's disaster, then began looting its goods, and finally they attacked the refugees. Such an attitude invited action on the part of God. Edom's catastrophe would be the result of divine intervention carried out through His own agents.

The Day of the Lord

The day of Jerusalem's destruction when Edom acted wickedly and the day of God's punishment on Edom, both point to the coming day of the Lord (verse 15). God holds responsible those who take advantage of others in their time of distress. The wrong done to others will return on the head of the wrongdoer. Yet God will not allow the punishment to go beyond the magnitude of the crime. Divine justice is also evident from the fact that He holds all nations, including Edom and Israel, accountable for what they have done. Verse 16 of Obadiah introduces the concept of God's anger through the figure of drinking from a cup. The Bible employs the image of a cup as a common metaphor for an individual's or a nation's destiny. Since God is just, He holds responsible those who take advantage of others in times of distress.

But Obadiah enlarges the picture of the divine cup to apply to all Edomlike nations. The prophet compares them to stubble and divine judgment to fire and flame. The hostile nations will drink to the full the cup of wrath, while salvation will come to those who stand in the place of God's deliverance, Mount Zion, on which the faithful focus their hope (cf. Joel 2:32). Obadiah sees Zion's holy mountain as standing in opposition to Edom's proud Mount Seir. Israel's kingdom will stretch from southwest (the Negev) to northeast (Gilead) with all the land in between (the fields of Ephraim and Samaria). The last verse in the book points to the end of history. The messianic king will reign over not just Israel but all the nations of the world symbolized by Edom. At the time of the end it will be evident to all people that the kingdom belongs to the Lord, the same One who had called Obadiah to be His spokesperson (see verse 1). God attaches His own authority to the prophetic pronouncement.

Obadiah affirms that the destruction of Jerusalem and its Temple did not result in His defeat. "Any intrusion of divine judgment in the history of redemption is evidence that God rules. The godly may take comfort in the hope that human powers will be brought down and that God's kingdom will come with power and salvation."[4] The prophetic book calls on God's people to have not passive but active hope in their Lord and His eternal kingdom on earth. On the wall of an old castle in Europe one can read the following words in Latin: *dum spiro, spero!* Translated, they mean "As long as I live, I have hope!" The apocalyptic vision of John the revelator applies the last verse from Obadiah's book to the very end of earth's history: "The kingdom of the world has become the kingdom of our Lord and of his Messiah, and he will reign for ever and ever" (Rev. 11:15). Thus the final message of the prophecy of Obadiah is one of victory and salvation. What more can the children of God today hope for?

---

[1] S. Kealy, *An Interpretation of the Twelve Minor Prophets of the Hebrew Bible*, p. 56.

[2] Samuel Pagan, "The Book of Obadiah: Introduction, Commentary, and Reflections," *The New Interpreter's Bible* (Nashville: Abingdon Press, 1996), vol. 7, p. 449.

[3] Based on the original Hebrew text.

[4] Willem A. VanGemeren, *Interpreting the Prophetic Word* (Grand Rapids: Zondervan Pub. House, 1990), p. 144.

Chapter 5

Messages From the Book of Jonah

In October 2010 a tsunami struck Indonesia's remote Mentawai Islands. A captain and his crew were on board a surfing charter boat anchored off a bay. Ten-foot-high waves formed a massive wall of white water and caused the boat to plow into another vessel that caught fire and burned completely down to water level. Fortunately all those on the two crafts survived the danger of drowning in the high waves. When later interviewed, the captain declared, "We were just hanging on for grim death. Everyone on board had been shaken—we all thought we were going to die. I have never experienced anything like this in my life. I can't get it out of my head. Those few moments when the tsunami struck keep replaying in my mind. We are glad to be alive and of some assistance to the people in the area. We are just glad to be alive."

The biblical prophet Jonah expressed his own joy of escaping the sure prospect of drowning. His prayer of thanksgiving became a living testimony to God's power and grace. Yet the same Jonah opposed God's willingness to extend divine grace to others. While the first two chapters of Jonah's book tell of the reluctant prophet's miraculous deliverance, the last two relate the deliverance of a repentant foreign city.[1] Jonah's book is so full of unexpected events that it has been called one of the "four strange books" of the Bible.[2] Although Jonah consists of only 48 verses, it is a veritable masterpiece among biblical books.

Jonah is probably the most widely known of the twelve prophets, because his story presents one of the best-loved narratives in the Bible. Although his background is shrouded in mystery, he turns out to be one of the most successful of all prophets. The book gives no precise information about the date of the events described in the story. The statement from 2 Kings 14:25 places the ministry of Jonah in the middle of the eighth century B.C. From it we learn that Jonah was an optimistic prophet from Galilee (rather than Judea) who lived and ministered during the long reign of

Jeroboam II. This king, according to biblical writers, did evil in the sight of the Lord. In spite of this, Jonah supported his ruler's territorial growth to the north and south, an expansion criticized by the prophet Amos (Amos 6:14). One could rightly argue that of "all [the] prophets to send to save foreigners, Jonah would be the least likely choice."[3]

Jonah's name in Hebrew means "dove." A text from Hosea insightfully portrays the northern kingdom of Israel, also called Ephraim, as a senseless and easily deceived dove. Hosea's description of Israel is strikingly similar to the story of Jonah:

"Ephraim is like a dove, easily deceived and senseless—
now calling to Egypt, now turning to Assyria.
When they go, I will throw my net over them;
I will pull them down like the birds in the sky.
When I hear them flocking together,
I will catch them" (Hosea 7:11, 12).

Jonah's book tells the story of someone who disobeyed God, then suffered partial consequences of his deed, yet in the process brought the message of salvation to others. Interpreters have approached the book in a variety of ways, but the best way to read Jonah is to take it as "a didactic story." Its overall themes are the urgency of repentance, the beauty of God's character, and the fact that salvation is a gift from the Lord. Because the book teaches repentance and divine forgiveness so clearly, the Jewish people read it on the Day of Atonement.

A Disobedient Prophet

The book opens with the customary formula "The word of the Lord came to . . . ," found in most prophetic books of the Bible and in particular used to describe God's call of Elijah (1 Kings 17). Although his book does not call Jonah a prophet, the text does imply such a title, and 2 Kings 14:25 confirms it. The command given by the Lord to Jonah son of Amittai consists in the original language of three short imperatives: "Rise! Go! Proclaim!" God tells the prophet to go to Nineveh, a city located on the eastern bank of the Tigris River.[4] The book calls Nineveh "the great city" or better yet, "greater Nineveh," because the designation included the region that surrounded it.[5] Jonah's task is to proclaim God's message *to* the people of this city and even *against* it. Their wickedness, just like that of Sodom and Gomorrah (Gen. 18:20, 21), has come up before God. The original word for "wickedness" could also be translated as "calamity," so it is possible that

Jonah's proclamation was a strong warning about a disaster or calamity that would strike that city.

Despite a clear command, Jonah does not obey God's instruction. Instead, he runs away. Unwilling to perform service for the Lord, he flees to evade his divine calling. Jonah's hometown was Gath-hepher, in the tribe of Zebulun, located just northeast of Nazareth in Galilee. Nineveh was in the east, so the prophet heads in the opposite direction to Tarshish, somewhere in the west. Nineveh was one of the capital cities of the Assyrians, a people of notorious cruelty. Assyria had harassed and exploited Israel and Judah for more than a century. Both Zephaniah and Nahum condemned Nineveh's arrogance and cruelty and announced its coming destruction (Zeph. 2:13-15; Nahum 3:1). In fact, the two short prophetic books of Jonah and Nahum are the only ones ending with a question, and both deal with the sins of Nineveh but in different or complementary ways. Jonah's book makes it clear that the prophet is not running away from Nineveh or its cruel inhabitants. Instead, he tries to flee from the presence of the God whose character he knows so well.

Jonah goes down to Joppa (modern Jaffa) on the Mediterranean coast and boards a ship bound for the west. Below deck he finds a comfortable place to rest. Yet the disobedient prophet has underestimated God's resolve to send him to Nineveh. He knows that God is loving, but he has yet to learn that the Lord will not stop short of anything in His plan to save the lives of His creatures. So He gets in Jonah's way by hurling a dangerous storm on the sea. In this way God counters the rebellious Jonah not in direct speech but rather in indirect action, because it was precisely what Jonah had done in response to God's command. Out of great fear that they might perish, the sailors sense a divine origin of the storm and turn to their deities for help. They also try to lighten the ship, since their prayers do not make the sea calm. It is also possible that they hurled their wares into the water in order to appease the stormy sea. As for Jonah, he was soundly asleep at the bottom of the ship. The original Hebrew text describes his sleep as being as deep as was Adam's when God took one of his ribs to create Eve (Gen. 2:21).

The captain of the ship commands Jonah to seek the presence of his God, not knowing that the prophet had actually been running away from the Deity. The captain's command "Get up and call!" sounds in the original Hebrew very much like what the Lord said at the beginning of the story (Jonah 1:2). Furthermore, his observation that "maybe he will take notice of us . . ." shows that although being a Gentile, he still knows too well that divine grace should not be taken for granted. In order to find the guilty person whose actions had led to the divine sending of the storm, the crew casts lots, and it singles Jonah out. The frightened seamen immediately bombard him with several short questions. In his response, Jonah identifies himself as a Hebrew who worships (literally "fears or respects") the Lord God of heaven. The title "Lord of Heaven" *(Baal Shamem)* was known among the Phoenician seamen. The more Jonah tells them about himself and his God, the better they understand the reason for the storm and consequently the more terrified they become.

Fully realizing the source of their trouble, they ask the prophet what they should do. Having no way to escape, he pronounces the verdict on himself: they should offer his life as sacrifice to spare their own. Not being willing to be responsible for Jonah's death, the seamen make one more attempt to bring the ship to safety. When that fails, they cry no longer to their gods but to the Lord Himself, not really knowing what to do next. We find much truth in the saying that oftentimes "human beings cannot claim God for their own ends, but they can cry out for salvation."[6] The sailors readily acknowledge God's absolute sovereignty, and in their prayers they transfer the responsibility for Jonah's life back onto the Creator-God. After they throw Jonah overboard, the sea becomes calm. The seamen worship the Lord and present Him with offerings and vows. Jonah's disobedience has, ironically, led Gentile people to worship the Lord. The reader cannot miss the sharp contrast between Jonah's negative behavior and the favorable description of the non-Hebrew sailors. But God does not let Jonah die. His intervention saves the prophet from a watery grave. A large fish swallows him, and his survival is a real miracle. Nature's obedience to God stands as a strong rebuke to Jonah's own disobedience.

At this point in the book the story shifts from prose to a prayer in poetry. Jonah's lasting legacy from his stay in the belly of the fish is a well-crafted psalm of thanksgiving. While people often call it a prayer of thanksgiving for deliverance of someone on the verge of drowning, we could also term it a song of praise composed by Jonah to his God. Relating Jonah's experience *before* the fish swallowed him, it is full of expressions from the book of Psalms. The song says that Jonah, falling into the sea, uttered a short prayer to God who answered it. Now the prophet thanks God for not letting the power of the grave *(sheol)* separate him from his Lord. He had gone down to Joppa, down to the boat, down into the waters of the sea, and down to the world of the dead. But the Lord saved him by bringing him up (Jonah 2:6). When the prophet had reached the lowest depth of the sea, God intervened and delivered him.

Jonah yet fears that he might go to a watery grave. Being still in the fish, he prays that God will fully deliver him from his present condition so that he can worship once again in the Temple. He recognizes that idol worshippers will only be disappointed in times of trouble, because lifeless objects cannot save them. But, Jonah declares, the situation is quite different for those who worship God. He therefore pledges to offer sacrifices and fulfill his vows to the only God who can save lives. The closing statement in the psalm ("Salvation comes from the Lord") is a fitting summary and conclusion of the entire song of praise (Jonah 2:9).

At the end of "three days and three nights" Jonah finds himself back on dry land. Thus "the God of Jonah is obviously active not only in human lives, but in the realm of nature as well. Not only can he speak and listen to people, but he is master of storms and big fish."[7] In three places in the Gospels (Matt. 12:38-42; 16:1-4; Luke 11:29-32) Jesus speaks about the sign of Jonah and ties the prophet's experience beneath the sea to His own impending death. Early Christian paintings in the catacombs portray Jonah as an emblem of resurrection.

A Successful Mission

God offers Jonah a fresh start. The Lord's command found in the beginning of chapter 3 is almost identical with the previous one given at the start of the book. The author makes it clear that the origin of Jonah's message is with the Lord, although he does not employ the standard formula of "thus says the Lord." This time Jonah obeys and goes to Nineveh, a city important to the Lord. Pointedly, the book does not refer to it as an "evil city." In Bible times the distance between Israel and Nineveh was about a month's journey. The "three days" (Jonah 3:3) that Jonah needs to complete his mission echo the three days and three nights that he spent in the fish. Jonah's proclamation can be condensed in no more than five words in Hebrew. After he walks and preaches for just a day, the results are astounding. He does not need to work hard before the whole city responds positively to his message (verse 5).

It is true that on the surface the prediction did not appear to present any hope of deliverance. Yet on a deeper level, the Ninevites welcomed the fact that God did not want to allow their destruction before forewarning them. Perhaps such a loving God would spare them completely if they truly repented. Their hopes prove true. Facing the threat of an imminent judgment, they immediately repent. The Ninevites trust God's message, something that the people of Israel have often failed to do. In contrast to the stubborn and rebellious Israelites described in Hosea and Amos, these non-Hebrew people appear ready to respond to God through fasting and repentance. The people of the ancient Near East regarded abstinence from food and putting on sackcloth as external signs of repentance (1 Kings 21:27; Esther 4:1; Joel 1:13, 14). All classes of people, including the king on the throne, now humble themselves before God. The all-inclusive statement "from the greatest to the least" *(merism)* suggests the inclusion of "male and female, royalty and commoner, nobility and peasant, aged and youth, powerful and powerless—indeed, all sorts and conditions of people."[8]

The king exchanges his royal robes for uncomfortable sackcloth and his throne for dust and ashes (Jonah 3:6). He and his nobles issue a decree addressed to both people and animals. Since the looming destruction threatens all, so all need to fast and turn to God. Their outward signs are to be accompanied by the right attitude, one that rejects violence and evil behavior. What is remarkable is that Nineveh's leaders acknowledge that God is not obliged to forgive. Recognizing that human actions do not dictate divine responses, they can only hope that their trust in God will spare them from perishing (verse 9). But the God of the Bible does not reject sincere repentance. Because of the people's willingness to change, He relents from punishing them the way He had previously planned. In doing so, He is acting in accordance with His holy and gracious character (Jer. 18:7, 8). Although the Ninevites did not necessarily convert to the lasting worship of the true God, their repentance was genuine and acceptable to Him. Jesus commended their faith and presented their repentance as a model to emulate. He predicted that Nineveh's attitude would at the end condemn the lack of faith among God's people (Matt. 12:39-41; Luke 11:29-32).

The success of Jonah's preaching goes beyond that of any other biblical prophet, yet he is not delighted by it but displeased. While he had greatly rejoiced in his own deliverance from death in the sea, Jonah now becomes angry (Jonah 4:1), because God has forgiven the Ninevites and allowed them to live. In his prayer he tells the Lord that divine readiness to forgive was the reason that he had tried to run away. "Whereas some prophets shrank from preaching because they saw no hope, Jonah refused because he knows there is hope. Whereas some prophets complained about the wrath of Yahweh (e.g., Jer 20:7-9), Jonah protests the love of God."[9] To Moses on Sinai the Lord revealed Himself as "the compassionate and gracious God, slow to anger, abounding in love and faithfulness, maintaining love to thousands, and forgiving wickedness, rebellion and sin" (Ex. 34:6, 7). It is astounding that God's compassion displeases Jonah so much that he wishes to die. He overlooks the fact that God in His grace had spared the prophet's own life.

The Lord reveals His reaction to Jonah's death wish through a couple rhetorical questions: "Is it right for you to be angry?" (Jonah 4:4). Although not coercive, the Lord is now persistent in dealing with Jonah. Acting as the prophet's guide and teacher, He approaches him with questions instead of commands. Like Elijah (1 Kings 19:4), Jonah wants to die, but God shows him the folly of self-centeredness. It indicates that the Lord wants to save not just Nineveh but also His prophet. Jonah's witnessing experience will become God's way of changing his heart. "The good news for angry Jonah is that God has mercy on *him*."[10] Poet Robert Frost aptly said: "After Jonah, you could never trust God not to be merciful again."

The prophet had found a place east of the city from which he had planned to observe the destruction of Nineveh. A makeshift shelter offered protection from the heat of the sun, but its leaves soon withered in the hot sun. Then the Lord provided a plant whose fresh leaves screened Jonah from the scorching heat. The prophet delighted in its shade. But the next morning a worm attacked the plant, and it shriveled. A hot east wind made Jonah very uncomfortable, and he became faint. Once again he desired to die like the withered plant (Jonah 4:8). Fortunately, Jonah does not have the last word in the story.[11] God seems determined to use events, "everything from a bush to a worm to a scorching east wind, to educate people like Jonah (and ourselves)."[12]

For a second time God reacts to Jonah's death wish with a question: "Is it right for you to be angry about the plant?" (verse 9). Who is more important: a multitude of people and cattle or a single plant? Moreover, can anyone put limits on God's mercy and forgiveness? Jonah seems so concerned for a small plant, yet he is indifferent—even hostile—toward so many people who bear God's image. And there were 120,000 of them! Moreover, the Lord also feels compassion for their animals. His attitude is so different from Jonah's whose quarrel in the story is not with the city but with God's character. Jonah cares only about the things that benefit him. He delights in the shade of plant, but when beaten by the sun he wants to die. "At odds with God, Jonah typifies those who see the divine attributes of justice and mercy as functioning for their own convenience; mercy for themselves, but justice for their enemies."[13] The end of the story makes God's prophet and His people look bad while presenting Israel's worst enemy, Assyria, in a positive light. "The irony of the gracious God who has such an ungracious prophet is clear."[14] Indeed, Jonah's book is a handbook on how *not* to be a prophet!

Jonah's story begins with a proclamation of judgment on the people of Nineveh, yet it ends with grace and salvation in behalf of that great city. Clearly, God pitied Nineveh not just because its people turned from evil, but also because of its size, ignorance, and even its animals. The Lord's desire to save goes beyond the boundaries of the chosen people, because to deliver the lost is His supreme commitment. The prophets taught that both human actions and God's freedom to act out of His loving heart will affect their predictions. The Lord said through Jeremiah: "If at any time I announce that a nation or kingdom is to be uprooted, torn down and destroyed, and if that nation I warned repents of its evil, then I will relent and not inflict on it the disaster I had planned" (Jer. 18:7, 8).

Readers of the Bible cannot help noticing some important parallels between the story of Jonah and the parable of the prodigal son (Luke 15:11-32). We can compare God to the loving parent and Nineveh to the prodigal child, while Jonah acts as the elder brother who resents the parental forgiveness and compassion. Both this parable and Jonah's book are left open-ended. We find ourselves in Jonah. In fact, we are him. "At once sympathetic toward and scornful of Jonah, we cannot help but be intrigued by his flight from God and his fight with God."[15] When God calls us to serve Him, we can respond in three ways. We can refuse to go, or we may go but be unwilling to change, or else we can go and be changed. And that is what God wants to happen to us. Mahatma Gandhi, that preeminent leader of India, once explained his philosophy of life in this way: "The best way to find yourself is to lose yourself in the service of others."

---

[1] D. Clark and J. Brunt, eds., *Introducing the Bible,* p. 418.

[2] Elias J. Bickerman, *Four Strange Books of the Bible* (New York: Schocken Books, 1967).

[3] Clark and Brunt, p. 417.

[4] The modern name for Nineveh is Mosul in northern Iraq.

[5] Just as the name Babylon was sometimes used in the sense of "Babylonia."

[6] Phyllis Trible, *The Book of Jonah: Introduction, Commentary, and Reflections,* The New Interpreter's Bible (Nashville: Abingdon, 1996), vol. 7, p, 502.

[7] J. Dybdahl, *Hosea-Micah,* p. 167.

[8] Trible, p. 516.

[9] *Ibid.,* p. 481.

[10] Dybdahl, p. 180.

[11] Trible, p. 522.

[12] S. Kealy, *An Interpretation of the Twelve Minor Prophets of the Hebrew Bible,* p. 61.

[13] T. Desmond Alexander, *Obadiah, Jonah, Micah: An Introduction and Commentary* (Downers Grove, Ill.: InterVarsity Press, 1988), p. 90.

[14] Dybdahl, p. 161.

[15] Clark and Brunt, p. 415.

Chapter 6

Messages From the Book of Micah

Outside of the United Nations building in New York stands a tall bronze sculpture made by the Russian artist Yevgeny Vuchetich and presented to the United Nations in 1959. The sculpture depicts the figure of a man holding a hammer aloft in one hand and a sword in the other, which he is making into a plowshare. The sculptor meant it to symbolize humanity's desire to put an end to war, and to convert the means of destruction into creative tools for the benefit of all. The title of the sculpture, "Let Us Beat Swords Into Plowshares," is based on Micah 4:3 (cf. Isa. 2:4).

It and two other verses from Micah's book have become familiar to readers of the Bible: the prophecy about Bethlehem as the birthplace of the future Messiah (Micah 5:2), and the response to the question of what the Lord requires of worshippers (Micah 6:8). But the book's rich content has much more to offer to a diligent student of the Bible. The Protestant Reformer John Calvin, for example, preached in Geneva no less than 38 sermons based on Micah. Although the prophetic book consists only of seven short chapters, the list of powerful messages and profound spiritual lessons it has to offer seems inexhaustible. The name Micah is an abbreviation of "Micaiah,"[1] which means "Who is like the Lord?" Such a rhetorical question implies an affirmative answer: There is no god like the Lord! We find a play on the name at the end of the book (Micah 7:18) in a hymn of praise to God's forgiveness and His faithfulness to the covenant promises.

Raised in the countryside, Micah was familiar with the poor in Judah. During King Hezekiah's spiritual reform he worked among the weak and the poor while Isaiah, who had a royal background, ministered among the wealthy. Since the book does not mention the name of Micah's father, it is safe to conclude that his background may have been that of one such poor family. Micah used the language of the common person, and his imagery was that of everyday life. As he preached to both Judah and Israel, he spoke against the moral corruption and economic exploitation that led to an outpouring of covenant curses and Samaria's eventual exile to Assyria. Micah condemned the prevailing idolatry (Micah 1:7; 5:13, 14) and predicted the destruction of Jerusalem and the Temple (Micah 3:12).

The time of Micah's ministry was one characterized by "political uncertainty, social unrest, and religious confusion."[2] He prophesied prior to and around the time of the Assyrian invasions of Palestine. During the chaotic eighth century Tiglath-Pileser III, whose Babylonian throne name was Pul (1 Chron. 5:26), came to power and began his incursions into Syria-Palestine. The Assyrian army erased the northern kingdom of Israel in 722 B.C. Twenty years later the Assyrian king Sennacherib destroyed 46 walled cities and besieged Jerusalem. He boasted of how he had shut King Hezekiah in Jerusalem "like a bird in a cage."

Most of what we know about Micah's life and background has to be inferred from the contents and tone of his writing. Like Amos, he was not a professional but a lay prophet (cf. Amos 7:14). Micah criticized the prophets who "give oracles for money" (Micah 3:11, NRSV). He predicted the loss of their prophetic gifts while reaffirming his own call to prophesy. False prophets could not balance God's mercy and justice, and that is why they led people into a false sense of security. Instead of being a counterculture, they became acculturated to the practices that Judah's leaders had adopted from the surrounding nations. But Micah's attitude was different. "Judging from the oracles he left behind, one assumes that Micah was a fiery preacher who defended the cause of the poor, often in forceful and graphic language."[3] Second Kings 17:16, 17 gives a short list of sins committed by the leaders and the people in Micah's time.

His ministry, combined with Isaiah's prophetic work, influenced Hezekiah, king of Judah, to introduce sweeping reforms. It saved Judah from the threat of complete destruction. Moreover, Micah's influence on the prophet Jeremiah's ministry later in Judah's history was remarkable. Just as Micah supported King Hezekiah's spiritual reform, so Jeremiah's ministry strengthened a similar movement under Josiah. Thus, one century after Micah's prophetic ministry, certain elders quoted a verse from his book (Micah 3:12) as a defense of Jeremiah's prophecy. In his Temple sermons (Jer. 7; 26) Jeremiah had predicted Jerusalem's destruction, and this led to his arrest. He escaped a death sentence thanks to the elders' speech and their citing of Micah (Jer. 26:17-24).

We could describe Micah's book as a collection or anthology of oracles, visions, and speeches. The book is mostly poetic with a few prose sections.

Its style employs frequent use of figures of speech and play on words. Literary forms (genres) include announcements of doom and salvation, oracles against foreign nations, disputation, lawsuits, funeral lament, prayer, hymns, and divine appearance (theophany). Some scholars consider the book to be the centerpiece of the twelve prophets since it contains in capsule form the message of all 12 of them. Micah spoke as someone shown the world through God's eyes. He said that because the Lord is just, He hates sin and will discipline His people. But there is hope because the same God is also forgiving and merciful. This perspective enabled Micah to see beyond present and future darkness. The prophetic rebuke becomes the channel of restoration and ultimate blessings. The book alternates between condemnation and hope. For this reason we could view Micah as the book of Isaiah in miniature. (Isaiah displays a similar pattern.)

The Lord Is Coming to Judge

Micah begins his book with the statement about divine origin of the revelation entrusted to him, one that God commissioned him to share with others. Filled with God's Spirit (Micah 3:8), he delivered the words that came to him from the Lord (Micah 1:1). In other words, we should read his book as God's Word. Micah's revelation originated in a specific context of time and place. He states that his ministry took place during the reigns of Jotham, Ahaz, and Hezekiah. In sharp contrast with Ahaz, Hezekiah was one of the few exemplary successes among the kings of Judah. Micah came from Moresheth Gath, a town located southwest of Jerusalem, a rural setting. Yet the importance of his message transcended that small and obscure location. All nations need to hear what God has to say. The Lord summons the whole earth to see His coming judgment.

The prophet announces that for a long time the Lord patiently observed people's sins, but now He is compelled to act. God is always present and active in the world, but during certain momentous times He will reveal His presence in powerful and unforgettable ways.[4] Such manifestations will suddenly cut their complacence short. The increase of sin on earth has affected the world of nature. The holy God comes from the Temple, His place of dwelling (cf. Hab. 2:20), to judge the earth's inhabitants. When the heavenly King enters the arena of His creation, it destabilizes the human environment. As mountains melt and low places split apart (Micah 1:4), a sense of awe and wonder prevails. All places, high and low (*merism*), crumble under God's feet. The forces of nature display themselves through volcanoes, earthquakes, and floods. The divine presence melts rocks and makes valleys to burst open. How can God's sinful people meet Him?

Israel's leaders, having lost their loyalty to God, have broken their covenant with Him. The word "therefore" found in Micah 1:6 begins the verdict issued by the sovereign Lord. The leaders of Samaria, the capital of the northern kingdom, have forsaken the living God for dead objects of worship. Micah said that idols would be totally destroyed when calamity comes. After the destruction of idols, the idol worshippers will face judgment. Samaria's wound is incurable. Its imminent destruction should serve as a warning of what would happen to Jerusalem. The prophet laments the destruction facing the towns of Judah. Since people normally built towns on hills, their destruction included pulling down their stone walls into the surrounding valley.

The vision of judgment produced a real tension in Micah's life, resulting in a personal lament (verses 8-16). As a true prophet, Micah does not rejoice in the looming destruction. Rather, he weeps for the wounded people of God. Prophets often used the lament to announce approaching disasters. The nation's Judge is here—at the city gate. The prophet goes around "barefoot and [partially] naked" as did Isaiah (Isa. 20) to show how the captives would be disgraced and humiliated. He howls like the jackals that one heard in the wilderness and wastelands, because that is what would become of his homeland. Micah is especially concerned for the cities and towns in Judah. Jerusalem is God's special child, "Daughter Zion."

The lament song presents wordplays between the names of the towns and their fatal destiny. Just to speak the names of these cities reveals something about their disastrous destiny.[5] *Beth-Ophrah*, for example, means "house of dust," and that is exactly what its future destiny would be. Rolling in the dust was an external sign of grief and self-abasement—caused in this case by a defeat. Invaders would conquer and strip town after town of its beauty and glory. Another city mentioned is Lachish, counted among the most prominent cities in the south. Sennacherib pictured its capture on the wall of a palace in Nineveh. As for Jerusalem, its wound is also incurable. Micah's message will serve as a witness and call to repentance to future generations.

The Assyrians forced Judah's leaders to pay a heavy tribute. Spiritual shepherds who once used to fleece their flock now find themselves fleeced by their conqueror. They will not be able to escape the coming exile. Just as David fled to Adullam from King Saul (2 Sam. 22:1), so the elite would from Jerusalem (Micah 1:15). But it would do no good. The "nobles of Israel" would find themselves carried into captivity. The last verse of chapter 1 lists the serious consequences of the nation's transgressions. The leadership had placed their security in their military power rather than in the Lord. To the prophets, prosperity was often a mixed blessing, because it occurred at the expense of the poor and weak. The leaders were complacent with their earthly kingdom, while they were apathetic to God's kingdom.[6] Micah calls the people of Jerusalem to join him in his lament (verse 16).

In chapter 2 the prophet describes more specifically the crimes of the people and the punishments that will follow. The word "woe" (Micah 2:1) implies the prospect of death threatening those who obtain through violence what does not belong to them. Filled with greed, the rich covet fields and seize them through force, dishonesty, or manipulation. In an agrarian society people's lives depend on their land. Without the ability to retain it, farmers would have to sell themselves into slavery to survive. People robbed of their land were also stripped of their identity. Micah vigorously defends the poor and sternly chastises the rich and powerful.[7] The wicked lie awake at night calculating how to steal other people's possessions. Instead of building a strong community that will care for the poor and vulnerable, the leaders took every opportunity to enrich themselves. They could do it because it was in their power to do so. With this type of situation, how could a society transcend greed and maintain fairness and justice?

The sentence will fit the crime, and the Lord Himself will carry it out. The consequences of evil actions will affect the future of the whole community. The day of the Lord will be the day of judgment when those who used to oppress their fellow countrymen would suffer the worst oppression possible. God was the owner of the land in Israel. That was why no one could ever sell it permanently, only lease it. Micah says that the Lord would take it back and hand it over to the enemy (cf. Deut. 28:49-68). Innocent persons such as women and children would suffer in the judgment along with the guilty. When in the future the remnant returns from exile to possess the land again, the greedy land-grabbers will no longer be present to have any share in it.

As happened during Jeremiah's ministry a century later, false prophets strongly opposed Micah's work. Self-appointed prophets warned him and his disciples not to prophesy. Their command (Micah 2:6) reminds one of Amaziah's warning to Amos at the shrine in Bethel (Amos 7:10-13). "False prophets may have actually been supporting, or at least silent in the face of, sinful land deals."[8] Instead of condemning, they condoned the sinful lifestyle. Later, around the time of the exile to Babylon, both Jeremiah (Jer. 23; 28) and Ezekiel (Eze. 13) spoke against false prophets who were selling their predictions for drinks and food (Micah 2:11). The common people had difficulty discerning between the prophets truly inspired by God and the impostors. But an important difference between them was that true prophets balanced love and justice. Their messages both confronted and comforted their audience. People should be wary of prophets who preach only peace (Jer. 28:8, 9). True prophets provided reproof and warning whenever the people violated God's covenant.

The false teachers downplayed the seriousness of sin, and they closed their eyes against social injustice and exploitation. They kept silent when someone seized the clothes of poor people or did not return before sunset a cloak taken in pledge. Thus the poor found themselves deprived of their only means to keep warm at night (Ex. 22:26, 27). Women and children, driven from their homes, lost their rightful inheritance (verse 22). With the same words used by the strong to oust the weak from the land, the Lord now pronounces sentence on the oppressors. As the wicked expelled the poor from the land, so will they be removed from God's presence (Micah 2:9)! Spiritual leaders were blind to the sin of the people and indifferent to injustice. As a consequence, they will receive a response from God that is as indifferent as was their own to the weak and poor. The egotistic attitude of the leaders had taught the people a self-centered way of life.

While Micah's messages condemned the attitude of rulers, priests, and prophets, his words did not lack of rays of hope, a welcome promise of grace. That is why Micah's book progresses from gloom to hope. Since the leaders had failed to be good shepherds of their people, the Lord now promises to be the Shepherd-King and deliver His own. After the Lord had driven the oppressor from His presence, the weak and suffering would find shelter in that same divine presence. Here is a clear promise about an eventual return from exile. The sign of that return will be Jerusalem's deliverance from Sennacherib's siege (2 Kings 19). The Shepherd-King will break the siege as He opens the gate and leads His people to freedom. He heads His joyful throng into victory.

The Lord commissioned Micah to declare His judgment on Judah's leaders, because the other prophets failed to confront and rebuke their greed, corruption, and exploitation. In chapter 3 the prophet turns to specific reasons for which God Himself decided to shepherd His people. The worst was the greed of the leaders, graphically depicted as a sort of cannibalism. The rulers cooked the poor like stew (Micah 3:1-3). The prophet compares the elite to impatient butchers who flay skin and tear flesh from God's people, breaking bones and chopping meat for the cooking pot. In their eagerness they devour flesh before it is even cooked.[9] Rulers, prophets, judges, and priests were all guilty of taking advantage of their flock. They failed to know divine teaching (Torah) and despised it. If ever they did use it, it was just for their own advantage. The leaders exercised their power not to defend the poor, but to protect the privileged.

Micah's false colleagues were prophets for profit. Their authority did not come from the Lord, but from corrupt human institutions, and their lying spirit had led the nation astray. The sole object of their work was how to get gifts and rewards. For this reason God would take away their gift of prophecy. Instead of visions, darkness would come upon them (verse 6) and they would endure public shame. Seers and prophets without visions or revelations would have no reason for being—they would have nothing to say. As for Micah, God's Spirit still spoke louder than money. Filled with great power, the prophet was not afraid to proclaim justice and the coming judgment. Micah 3:8 is the only verse that describes his call to prophesy. Courage, conviction, and dependence on God characterized his ministry. His prophecy was effective, because both the people and King Hezekiah repented, and thus the disaster did not occur when expected but was instead delayed (Jer. 26:18, 19).

In ancient Israel the ultimate responsibility for justice resided in the person of the king who had been anointed to execute God's will in the land. The Lord now calls the national ruler and his associates to listen to Him. They had built their prosperity through exploiting the poor and denying or violating basic rights to life and prosperity. Wickedness and bloodshed went unpunished. The sages held back their counsel, the priests ignored the Torah, and the prophets did not pass along God's messages. Money loomed more important than ethical responsibility.

People believed that because the Lord was in their midst no disaster could strike them (Micah 3:11). Like Jeremiah's contemporaries, they trusted in the physical building of the Temple more than in the God of the Temple (Jer. 7). They believed that Zion, the city of God, could never fall, because it symbolized God's kingdom on earth and the Lord's lasting covenant with David (Ps. 46:4, 5). But Micah said that Jerusalem would become a heap of rubble. The Temple hill would lose its divine presence. Instead of calling the Temple "the house of the Lord," Micah now refers to it as merely "house." The Lord would give Jerusalem over to destruction because of the mistreatment of the widows, orphans, aliens, and the poor in its midst.[10]

Restoration Under a Just Ruler

Chapter 4 of Micah opens with a sudden shift from the desolation of the old Jerusalem and its Temple to the glory of the new city and the elevation of its Temple mount. In the blink of an eye, everything has changed. The vision is a breath of fresh air. Jerusalem's Temple mount, the center of God's presence on earth, will tower above all others, and all people will recognize its importance. The vision reported in Micah 4:1-7 echoes Isaiah 2:1-5 with some variations. Describing God's healing, community building, and covenant restoration, it balances the harsh yet necessary words of chapters 1-3.[11] The Lord, in the end, will be recognized as the Sovereign over the nations, and all people will eagerly draw on His Word. He will reestablish justice, peace, and security in the world. Mutual trust will replace wars. Only the Lord can guarantee lasting prosperity and justice (cf. Dan. 2).

Rising from its ashes, Zion towers in a spiritual sense above all other mountains. It draws to itself many non-Hebrew people. Those not yet walking in God's name would desire to do the Lord's will. The nations of the world come willingly to learn about God so that they also may walk in His paths. God's message to the nations consists of His unchanging Word and a new way of relating to one another in justice and peace. The prophet hears the nations inviting one another to go up and hear God's Word.[12]

God will raise up the Temple mountain to bridge the gulf between Him and the world. Many from the nations join the Hebrew pilgrims to Zion. The New Jerusalem will become the center of worship for the whole earth. Gentile pilgrims will stream to Zion, seeking God's will and putting it into practice in their lives. Hearts transformed by divine instruction will no longer desire wars but rather a lasting worldwide peace. Humanity will use the earth's resources to cultivate life not death. The messianic kingdom will be a universal rule of peace. People will make weapons of death into tools to grow food for life.[13] Contrary to the ways of the nations, Micah affirmed that he and the faithful remnant would persist walking in the way of the Lord (Micah 4:5).

Greed, covetousness, and exploitation of others would give way to peace, love, sharing, and prosperity for all. Such is the nature of God's kingdom in contrast with earthly kingdoms. The Lord of hosts, whose preferred ways of resolving problems have always been those of peace and understanding, will guarantee the new reign of harmony. The idyllic picture of tranquillity and prosperity in the Bible lands was to be able to sit under one's own vine and fig tree. The vision of Zion's future glory serves as an inspiration to the people of God to walk in the ways of the Lord that He had presented to them long ago. The Lord will regather His faithful remnant, and His reign will know no end. Those society once cast off will now constitute God's remnant. The Lord promises to eliminate the fear, mistrust, and greed so deeply rooted in sinful human nature.

Although God promises much better times, His people will have to endure great trouble before that hope will be realized. In the day of the Lord even "the lame" will be brought into the restored people of God (verse 6), a promise that reminds us of Jacob's experience at Jabbok (Gen. 32:22-32), which resulted in a great blessing. The weak and the oppressed are God's remnant that will inherit the land. With Jerusalem's dominion restored, its leaders will fully care for their flock. Daughter Zion will once again be a fortified tower from which the Shepherd-King will offer protection to God's people. Zion's future glory should motivate the people to godly living in their own time (verses 9-13). Micah's words of hope took seriously the reality of present suffering. The problem of sin had no easy solution or a quick fix, because sins make His work more difficult. Yet in spite of this, His intentions toward His people are always good (cf. Gen. 50:20).

The divine ruler knows what is best for His people. His act of disciplining His children is not intended to be penal but remedial. Zion's sufferings open the door of hope to salvation and victory. Scripture uses the pain experienced by a woman in labor as the standard metaphor to portray God's people as they wait for the coming Messiah. The promised kingdom of heaven comes through trials—not away from them. And even those carried into exile will return from Babylon. Such promises greatly comforted a nation under threat from enemies who intended to desecrate God's holy Temple. God would judge them as sheaves that have been sifted on the threshing floor (cf. Isa. 21:10). The speech of the unrepentant nations contrasts with that of the repentant peoples reported in the beginning of the chapter. Zion uses agricultural tools (Micah 4:13) as instruments of war to defend itself. After God's victory over the hostile nations, the Lord is crowned as ruler of all the earth.

Like the preceding chapter, Micah 5 also progresses from the present distress to future salvation. While Judah's king may be defeated and humiliated, the ideal king, the Messiah, is victorious and glorified. The movement is from suffering to salvation, from defeat to victory. The opening word "now" (NRSV) introduces Jerusalem's present difficulties under the Assyrian siege and threat against King Hezekiah. The Assyrian rod appears too strong when measured against the remnant of Israel's army. There are two ways to translate Micah 5:1: "Marshall troops!" or "Walled within a wall." Both fit the context and relate to the situation in 701 B.C. since Micah uses the first person plural "us" in the verse. The prophet summons the people to marshal or assemble their troops in response to the advancing army. But it is a time of desperation, and the people are defenseless. God's chosen ones have to endure defeat and watch their leader abused. Judah's situation is as humiliating as the blows that strike the face of a helpless person (cf. Job 16:10; Ps. 3:7; Isa. 50:6; Lam. 3:30). God's plan was that the Messiah would rule the nations with a rod of iron (Ps. 2:9). Yet Judah's ruler is struck on the cheek and deeply insulted.[14]

The good news, though, is that punishment is never God's last word. "The movement in Micah and throughout Scripture is always from judgment to forgiveness, from punishment to mercy, from suffering to hope."[15] The word "but" (Micah 5:2) marks a sudden reversal. Although the monarch from Jerusalem is humiliated, the future Messiah from lowly Bethlehem is glorified. Located between Judah's two important cities of Jerusalem and Hebron, Bethlehem will be honored to be the birthplace of the future Son of David. Ephrata was the name of a region in Judah (Ruth 1:2), and it means "fruitful." The new ruler will be strong because his strength will come from the Lord. His reign will not be in his own power or might, and will extend to the ends of the earth.

Thus a new ruler arises from an unlikely place. The Bible never lists Bethlehem among fortified cities. In many ways it was considered as insignificant.[16] But later it became special because it was the home of King David, the ruler who united Israel and led it to its golden age. People expect great personalities from great places, but it is not so with God. The Messiah's birth will seem as unexpected as was the choice of David to be king. A seemingly insignificant place will be the home of the most exalted person. Through His prophets God gave specific information about the distant future. The New Testament would later quote Micah 5:2 to show its fulfillment in the birth of Jesus Christ whose origins go back to King David

(Matt. 1:1, 2). The work of the Messiah will be to fulfill God's purpose on earth. He will reign forever in line with the Lord's eternal covenant with David (2 Sam. 7:8-16).

Jerusalem's deliverance will come in the future, not now. The time of salvation is not yet. Although at present the people feel that they have been given to the enemy (Micah 5:3), they must have faith and hope in God to send the new ruler. Abandonment in the form of exile will first take place. Daughter Zion will go through the pains of labor before the Messiah comes. The faithful remnant will join the repentant people who follow the Messiah. Micah portrays God as the shepherd of His people (Micah 2:12; 4:6-8; cf. Ps. 23; Eze. 34). Jesus also identified Himself as the good shepherd (John 10). The promise from Micah 5:2 also looks forward to Christ's second coming when the reign of God will finally be realized in all its glory. The Lord promises to act, protect, and restore. We still wait for the complete fulfillment although Jesus already fulfills the role of the new ruler. He came not in Micah's time but in God's time. His grace, power, and peace sustain us in times of pain and grief.[17] The birth of the Savior does not spare us from our problems but gives us assurance that God is with us in our deepest pain. His rule will be over a kingdom so vast that it will have no borders. He will shepherd His flock in the power of God.

The defeat of the enemy will bring eternal peace and prosperity. The saved community will have no lack of leaders (Micah 5:5, 6) to stand up to the enemies, symbolized here by Assyria. The returning remnant will be the agent of God's reign among the nations. Their presence will bring blessings to others just as Jacob's family brought blessings to the Egyptians. Dew and rain symbolize blessings sent from heaven. The remnant is also comparable to an invincible lion, the king of the animal world. Thus the presence of Israel's remnant among the nations will bring blessings like dew from heaven and victory as strong as the lion. So the concept of a remnant includes both a threat and a promise: threat because many people will perish and only a few will survive, and promise because God will not allow a complete destruction. As for the oppressors, He will punish them. Vengeance belongs to Him alone. He promises to protect His kingdom.

The day of the Lord will bring cleansing to God's people and the removal of idols, pride, and self-confidence. Idols and images cannot impart life. Created objects can never take place of the Creator. Micah links idolatry to magic and divination brought to Israel from Mesopotamia (see

Isa. 2:6-8). While some people put their faith in horses and other military power (Ps. 20:7), the remnant will trust in the Lord God. Their prosperity depends on their faithfulness. If Israel is to be the role model to the nations, it first needs to be purified and reject all compromise with evil. The new Shepherd will protect His people from all Assyria-like enemies and lead them to places of secure dwelling.

Hope Shines Through Darkness

As he begins the final section of his book, Micah restates the divine origin of his message. He returns to the present state of the nation, its sins, and the resulting crisis. The passage presents the drama of a courtroom scene. People go to court when an important rule has been broken. The prophet brings charges against the people in the context of a lawsuit. Thus God puts His people on trial. The lawsuit serves to establish justice and truth. The divine courtroom is surrounded by mountains and hills that from the beginning of history have seen everything and can serve as reliable witnesses. Micah is God's spokesperson as the Lord accuses Israel of breaking the covenant with Him. He brings His charge against the whole community (cf. Isa. 1:2, 3; Jer. 2:4-13; Hosea 4:1-6).

The tone of God's voice betrays hurt and pain, because the relationship with the people He loves has shattered. He asks what has gone wrong between them. When people are disobedient and need to be punished, God feels pain (Micah 6:3). Through His questions the Lord defends His innocence by inviting the nation to testify against Him with a list of specific accusations. Has He done anything wrong or has He burdened His people so much that they felt forced to betray Him? The Lord then answers His own questions by reciting His saving acts in behalf of Israel since the day they left Egypt. In Micah as in Isaiah, God was weary of meaningless sacrifices and other forms of empty rituals.

In spite of the broken relationship, God still calls Israel "My people." The expression reveals His still affectionate feelings toward them. The nation has wronged God, the one who brought them out of Egypt. He who delivered His people from oppressive slavery has become burdensome to them. Yet the Lord did not allow Balaam to curse Israel. Because of His promises to Abraham, He turned the enemy's curses into blessings. He also parted the waters of the Jordan so that Israel could cross over (verse 5). As they remembered such sacred stories people could closely identify with them and apply them to their lives.

Israel acknowledges its guilt and asks what act of service can lead to forgiveness (verse 6). Would quality or quantity of sacrifices win God's favor? Year-old calves were more valuable than newborn ones. The first offer is a normal amount of sacrifice, but then it increases with each line of the passage, ending in hyperbole as to how to make things right with God. What about the most costly offering imaginable: child sacrifice? Although forbidden in Israel (Lev. 18:21; 20:2-5; Deut. 12:31; 18:10), human sacrifice was practiced by some individuals (2 Kings 3:27; 16:3; Jer. 7:31; Eze. 16:20, 21), including Ahaz (2 Chron. 28:3) and Manessah, son of Hezekiah (2 Kings 21:6). The implication of the progression is that no sacrifice offered by Israel can restore the broken relationship. But what can people do in worship to make things right with the Lord? God says that it is more than just worship—it is about living out the response to His grace.

The sentence spelled out by God is not punitive but restorative. He wants worship to be the grateful response to His forgiveness. The words from Micah 6:8 remind us of those of Moses in Deuteronomy 10:12: "And now, Israel, what does the Lord your God ask of you?" The answer includes the word "what" seen in the questions in Micah 6:3-5. In other words, "*What* fault did your ancestors find with Me?" The same word appears in the question about *what* would please God. Now God discloses *what* He has shown human beings from the beginning. The moral aspect of the prophetic proclamation was often expressed through the word "good," which encapsulates God's instruction for living (Amos 5:14, 15; Micah 3:2).

The three-part answer consists of an action (doing), an attitude (loving), and a relationship (walking with). An ancient Jewish rabbi said that Micah reduced the 613 laws of the Torah of Moses to only three principles. To do justice means to act in fairness in all aspects of life and society. The stress is not just on speaking for but doing justice. The requirement is relational and ethical. To act justly means to use one's power to help the weak. In the Bible the word "justice" *(mishpat)* includes whatever is in conformity with the Torah. Thus to love mercy requires developing a genuine attitude of generosity and grace. The Hebrew word for "mercy" *(hesed)* also describes acts of kindness. It combines loyalty and love, qualities vital in those types of relationship in which the parties are not equal. Mercy in the Bible has to do with love, loyalty, and faithfulness.

As we have noted already, "walking" is the standard biblical metaphor for living. To walk with God means to live in conformity with His truth and will and to have a continuing personal relationship with Him.

The believers should make God the center of their lives. Scripture some-times used "humbly" synonymously with "wisely" or "prudently" (cf. Prov. 11:2) and as an opposite to "proudly" (Micah 2:3). Our daily life is like a walk with God as our constant companion who expects more than out-ward acts of piety. He wants a dedication of our whole lives. The moral principles are eternal, and to obey them is more important than gifts (1 Sam. 15:22; Isa 1:11-17; Jer. 7:1-15; Hosea 6:6; Amos 5:21-24). Supe-rior to sacrifices and offerings is love toward God and one's neighbor. True faithfulness to the Lord is evident in the integrity of a just, gentle, and humble walk with God. Like the other biblical prophets, Micah teaches that no acts of worship can replace this (Amos 5:14, 15; Hosea 12:6; Isa. 1:16, 17; Zech. 7:7-10). The life and ministry of Jesus Christ is the best il-lustration of the three principles listed in Micah 6:8.

The prophet then says that people have not lived up to God's standard (verse 9). If they continue doing the same, they will become the targets of covenant curses such as famine, drought, pestilence, and war. Since the na-tion has failed to conform to God's will as spelled out in verse 8, it will have to die. God's call to respect Him has fallen on deaf ears. Instead of acting justly, merchants have been using false measures and scales (verses 10, 11). The prophet describes the powerful elite of Jerusalem as violent and dis-honest. They bend the rules to their advantage (verse 12). The divine judge pronounces the sentence on the oppressor: disease, hunger, destruction of the land, and inability to have children. Instead of walking with God, the people wandered in the ways of the wicked kings such as Ahab, whose name became a byword for idolatry and forceful confiscation of property from others (verse 16).

As Micah searched throughout the land, he could find no godly people (Micah 7:2). His lament song (cf. Micah 1:8, 9) begins with the exclama-tion "What misery is mine!" (Micah 7:1). Acting in the Lord's behalf, the prophet acts as a farmer who looks for grapes and figs, the fruit of his hard labor, but finds none (verse 1; cf. Gen. 18; 19; Isa. 5:1-7; Jer. 5:1; Zeph. 1:12). Searching for a faithful and upright person is as disappointing as finding no fruit in the vineyard or orchard. Micah can find only evildoers who take bribes, misuse power, and pervert justice. He agonizes over the deplorable state of both public and private life. The rulers and judges have all fallen short of the standard of justice. They lie in wait and weave nets to hunt their victims (Micah 7:2-4). Anarchy expels respect and trust in soci-ety and love in the family. One can no longer trust even a close friend or a lover. Each person fights for his or her own interests and survival (verses 5, 6). As God's watchman Micah warns of the approaching judgment.

Yet even in the midst of such tumult the prophet still anticipates the salvation promised so long ago (verse 7). God is his only reason for hope. Micah claims divine justice and mercy as he waits for the Lord to do something about the situation. Commentators have called the passage from Micah 7:8-17 a "song of confidence." God's daughter Zion has been humiliated and defiled. The enemy has mockingly demanded, "Where is the Lord your God?" But despite her defeat she declares her confident trust in God. Her suffering is only for a period of time after which the enemy will be put to shame. Sitting in darkness she confesses that the Lord is her only source of light. Her punishment is well deserved but so will be the righteous judgment on her enemy. He will be trampled on as the mire in the streets.

Daughter Zion's confession prompts a message of hope (verses 11-13). In the future her city walls will provide protection to the refugees who look for safety. Like a sheepfold, Zion will offer a shelter to the weak. The offer of salvation will go beyond Israel's borders into the whole world. The prophet can see how from everywhere people are on the move toward Jerusalem (cf. Micah 2:1-5). The prophet compares the beauty of the land to Mount Carmel. It will be as green as Bashan and Gilead, two fertile regions lying east of the Jordan River. In Micah's time Assyria had seized them, but the day of the Lord would restore all those territories to God's kingdom.

Micah entreats the divine Ruler to protect and provide for His people as shepherds care for their flocks. Wonders from long ago will come to pass again. The prophet asks God to perform once more the miracles from the time of the Exodus. Formerly hostile nations who have been so humbled that they lick the dust, now give up their wicked ways and seek the Lord. Thus the restoration of the people to their promised land will have a worldwide impact. Forgiving and pardoning the remnant, God will fulfill the covenant promises given to Abraham and Jacob. The divine Shepherd will lead His flock to places of safety.

The song of confidence transforms into one of victory (Micah 7:18-20). The prophet plays on his name (which means "Who is like the Lord?") to show God's incomparable character. No deity can compare with the merciful and forgiving God! None can pardon sins like the Lord. Thus Micah's name became symbolic of the restoration. God will forgive all aspects of wrongdoing: sins, transgressions, and iniquities (cf. Dan. 9:24). In the beginning of Israel's history the Lord hurled the enemy into the sea (Ex.

15) and so saved His people. The same God will at the end cast the transgressions of His people into the depths of the sea. God's people find hope for the future in remembering what He has done in the past. His love and mercy never fail (Ex. 34:6). The Lord will truly fulfill His promises made so long ago. They will not be broken. Micah proclaimed that God is just and righteous, but in the end forgiveness, mercy, and hope have the last word.[18]

An old church building in Pennsylvania has a "peace window." The stained-glass window features children looking on as a blacksmith beats cannon into plowshares. It is a call to be at peace with God and live in harmony with one another. To work for justice and peace, to piece together our common brokenness, is to do God's work. The last verse in Micah's book is one of the finest descriptions of God's grace, showing that in His very nature lies "a commitment to the future well-being of his people, a future characterized by divine protection, provision, and peace."[19]

The Lord expects His church to bear witness to His new creation and to work toward the reestablishment of God's kingdom and redemption of all creation. "In the midst of the gloom and judgment, we must remember that God has a future planned that is far better than anything we have ever known."[20] Micah's message of hope in God needs to be proclaimed and lived. Too many people in our world have heard only about the punishing God. They also need word of the loving and forgiving side of the Savior— that divine forgiveness is as deep as the sea.

---

[1] An alternative Hebrew form was *Mica-yahu*. We should not confuse Micah with another prophet named Micaiah son of Imlah, who hailed from the northern kingdom at the time of King Ahab (1 Kings 22; 2 Chron. 18).

[2] D. Clark and J. Brunt, eds., *Introducing the Bible*, p. 295.

[3] C. Aaron, *Preaching Hosea, Amos, and Micah*, p. 92.

[4] Daniel J. Simundson, "The Book of Micah: Introduction, Commentary, and Reflections," *The New Interpreter's Bible* (Nashville: Abingdon Press, 1996), vol. 7, p. 544.

[5] *Ibid.*, p. 548.

[6] W. Van Gemeren, *Interpreting the Prophetic Word*, p. 152.

[7] Aaron, p. 94.

[8] J. Dybdahl, *Hosea-Micah*, p. 200.

[9] Clark and Brunt, eds., p. 298.

[10] The tradition of the Jewish scribes (*Massorets*) regarded the prediction about the

fall of Jerusalem and the destruction of the Temple (Micah 3:12) as marking the center of the Book of the Twelve Prophets.

[11] Aaron, p. 101.

[12] The Jewish liturgy recites Micah 4:2 when the Torah scroll is taken from the ark to be read: "For instruction shall go forth from Zion."

[13] Aaron, p. 105.

[14] During the New Year's festival *(Akitu)* in Babylon the priest would strike the king on the cheek in a ritual that was to show the king's humiliation before the god Marduk.

[15] Simundson, p. 569.

[16] When Joshua 15 defines the boundaries of the various tribal allotments and lists the cities of Judah, Bethlehem was not considered important enough to be mentioned.

[17] Aaron, p. 114.

[18] S. Kealy, *An Interpretation of the Twelve Minor Prophets in the Hebrew Bible,* p. 103.

[19] Clark and Brunt, p. 294.

[20] Dybdahl, p. 208.

Chapter 7

Messages From the Book of Nahum

About two centuries after Nineveh's destruction a Greek army general passed by a pile of ruins located on the eastern side of the river Tigris. He asked if any one of the thousands of soldiers accompanying him knew the name of the city that once stood there. Not a single man could tell him that it was the remains of the great city of Nineveh, the capital of the Assyrian Empire. One of the greatest cities from ancient times now lay almost completely forgotten. The fall of the city of Nineveh, must have been the most important political event in the time of the prophet Nahum.

The name "Nahum" means "comfort" or "consolation," and it appears only twice in the Bible (Nahum 1:1; Luke 3:25). Its longer form ("Nehemiah," "the Lord is my consolation") occurs more frequently. The prophet's name fittingly expresses the message of his book: the Lord will comfort His oppressed people and bring an end to their suffering. Thus Nahum's prophecy presents God's answer to injustice and oppression.

The prophet's hometown was Elkosh, probably located in Judah. An ancient tradition, however, places Elkosh north of Nineveh (modern Mosul), the traditional site of the tomb of Nahum, a place long visited by Christian, Jewish, and Muslim pilgrims. On the other hand, since the name Capernaum in Galilee literally means "the town of Nahum," Jerome identified it with Elkosh. Despite those two traditions, scholars think that Elkosh was located southwest of Jerusalem. As for Nahum's time, he most likely ministered in the seventh century B.C., prior to the fall of Nineveh in 612 B.C. A Jewish tradition claims that he prophesied during the reign of King Manasseh.

Nahum's book is only 47 verses long and, just like Obadiah's short prophecy, it is addressed to a foreign city. Its topic is the fall of Nineveh at the hands of a military coalition of Medes and Babylonians. The prophecy came in response to the Assyrian oppression of Israel that had lasted for centuries.[1] Some scholars consider Nahum the most violent book in the Bible. It is important, however, to state that the message proclaimed by Nahum was not so much against Assyria or Nineveh as it was against oppression and evil. In Nahum Nineveh is both a historical city, the capital of the Assyrian Empire, and also a symbol of the sinful earthly oppression that God hates and promises to bring down.

The book focuses on God's character and His exercise of power and justice in the world. It offers a message of encouragement to His people. Nahum's book teaches that God will not let the wicked go unpunished. Knowing that He will bring evil to a definite end gives us great comfort. So the book contains a prophecy about the destruction of the oppressor and relief for the suffering. The Lord promises to stop the tyranny under which His people live. Isaiah had said that God used Assyria like a hired razor, yet He would punish it for its excessive cruelty (Isa. 7:20; cf. 10:24). The prophetic prediction came to pass when the Medes and Babylonians destroyed Nineveh and left it to become a pile of ruins.

The ancient Greek translation of the Old Testament known as the Septuagint places Nahum after the book of Jonah. Both books talk about Nineveh, the greatest city of the time, and both books end with a rhetorical question. Jonah's preaching in Nineveh resulted in repentance. But Nineveh's repentance did not last for a long time. Its people gradually returned to their evil ways. The Assyrians were notorious for their brutal use of power and endless cruelty. An Assyrian king, for example, boasted of how he covered the city wall with human skin. Another one bragged of how he erected a pyramid of human heads in front of an enemy city. Assyrian reliefs pictured bodies impaled on sticks and soldiers dragging captives by lip rings. The empire had carried the northern kingdom of Israel into exile in 722 B.C., and later its army marched King Manasseh of Judah off with a hook in his nose (2 Chron. 33:11). The Assyrian monarch once proudly said: "Shall I not deal with Jerusalem and her images as I dealt with Samaria and her idols?" (Isa. 10:11).

Some have misunderstood Nahum's message and labeled it as "self-serving nationalistic prophecy." Few preach from the book, and some readers of Scripture frankly admit they wish Nahum were not in the Bible. Indeed, the book has been a cause of embarrassment to many. Others, however, have taken a quite different approach and have called it a brilliant ode of triumph filled with vivid imagery, splendid metaphors, keen sense of irony.[2] The book's literary style is comparable to other biblical passages of the highest poetic quality. The book contains four judgment oracles, each ending with Judah's salvation (Nahum 1:12-15; 2:1-13; 3:1-7, 8-13). We might summarize Nahum's message as: God, who is faithful, has not abandoned His people. The enemy, though powerful, will not prevail forever, because God's power is still greater. That is why Nahum could confidently announce Nineveh's downfall. The day of the Lord would put an end to the Lord's enemies and offer protection to His people.

The Day of Vengeance

Nahum is the only prophet who named his writing "the book of vision," intending to say that he wrote God's revelation on a scroll.[3] The original word for "vision" or "revelation" may describe a prophecy concerning a non-Hebrew nation (for example, Isa. 13:1; 15:1). Sennacherib made Nineveh the capital city of Assyria. In the Bible the empire came to symbolize all of the enemies of God's people. Nahum's prophecy universally applies the Lord's attitude toward evil to any nation—including His own people. While God used Assyria to be His "rod" against Israel, He still held the empire's people accountable for their sinful actions.

Since Nahum's book describes the victory of the Lord against Assyria, chapter 1 opens with a hymn of praise to God's character (Nahum 1:2). The passage applies to the present situation the key text about the Lord's character as revealed to Moses on Mount Sinai (Ex. 34:6, 7). The hymn affirms the Lord's cosmic supremacy and control.[4] It portrays God's universal power and the justice evident in His dealings with the nation of Assyria.

This hymn is the key to the interpretation of the whole book. It portrays the Lord acting out of His great zeal. Verse 2 of chapter 1 implements the triple use of the expression "the Lord's vengeance." God is patient and delays His judgment, but He is now ready to pass sentence on the oppressor. Opportunities to repent may be many, but not endless. In other words, God's patience has its limits. It lasts for a long time, but not forever. Unlike when Jonah preached in the city, this time Nineveh had crossed a point of no return, and repentance was no longer an option.

God's zeal and patience do not negate each other (Nahum 1:3). Divine jealousy expresses its zeal in order to maintain the relationship with His people. The Lord is a warrior who promises to defend His people, a teaching that appears constantly throughout the Bible. The sea and the rivers dry up at the Lord's rebuke, while the mountains shake. God manifests His power in storm, earthquake, and other ways in which He can reverse His creation back to chaos. The original Hebrew text uses four different terms to describe God's anger (verse 6). Faced with God's awesome power that melts mountains, Nahum asks, "Who can endure the heat of his anger" (NRSV)? No created being can withstand His wrath and indignation. The purpose of divine anger is the removal of evil. The psalmist says that the Lord loves those who hate evil (Ps. 97:10).

Although God exhibits His wrath against evil, He is also a stronghold, high place, and refuge from the flood for His own people. But only those who actually seek His protection in time of trouble will find shelter in Him. To the humble, the Lord is good and a refuge in times of trouble (Nahum 1:7). The last section of Nahum 1, more than any other part of the book, abounds with words of comfort. Assyria's plots will come to nothing, because they are not strong enough to oppose God's power. When He intervenes, the Assyrians will perish like fire-consumed stubble (verse 10). God's dual verdict brings hope to Judah and an end to Assyria. The yoke of oppression will shatter. Normally the Bible regards the yoke as an instrument of service, but here it symbolizes subjugation. The oppressor will be buried without descendants (verse 14). God will destroy Assyria's temples and many idols such as those of Ashur, Sin, Shamash, Bel, Nebo, Nergal, and Ishtar.

The last verse of Nahum 1 contains a message of the good tidings of hope and peace in the land of Judah. A herald will bring to the nation the welcome news of deliverance from evil. The people will celebrate a feast of thanksgiving, because the Lord is acting for the salvation of His people. He will cut off the enemy completely, and it will be seen no more. His people will rejoice in the victory. The proclamation of the Lord's triumph is good news for Judah. The use of the name "Jacob" (Nahum 2:2) in the context shows that a renewal of the whole nation of Israel is in view. God summons all people to celebrate His victory over the enemy.

The End of the Oppressor

Nahum 1:15 describes Judah's joy at its restoration and freedom from oppressors and marauders, leading to a vivid and artful portrayal of the battle before the fall of Nineveh (Nahum 2:1-13).[5] The chapter opens with an ironic call to the Assyrian army to defend their city. In the eyes of many people Nineveh appeared invincible. A wide protective wall around made it virtually impregnable. Yet the prophet says that no amount of preparation will help the city withstand the attacks. God will carry out His judgment on Nineveh through a human enemy whose goal is to scatter its inhabitants. The description of the battle is so detailed that it reads like an eyewitness account (verses 3, 4). The attacking army is clothed in red and scarlet, which meant expensively dyed uniforms. The shiny metal fittings of the chariots flash in the sun and have the appearance of torches.

Nineveh's soldiers prove unable to defend the city (verse 5). Its gates are open, and the palace collapses. The invaders plunder the treasury and take the people captive. Enemy soldiers loot the temple of its idols. Nineveh is devastated, desolate, and destroyed. It is possible that a flood contributed to Nineveh's fall (verse 6), but more likely the waters serve here as a metaphor for the conquering flood of the enemy. Fear and terror fall on all the city's population. The standard used in judgment is "measure for measure." What the Assyrians once did to others now happens to them. The reader can only conclude that God is indeed active in human history.

Even the well-disciplined Assyrian army is in disarray, and every soldier tries to escape. No one turns back, but all flee (verse 8). Nineveh has become like a pride of lions without lairs (verses 11-13). Assyrian wall reliefs often portrayed their kings hunting lions. Lions accompany the image of Ishtar, the Mesopotamian goddess of love and war. These symbols of courage have disappeared from their den. Addressing this great military power, the Lord declares: "See, I am against you" (NRSV)! When confronted by the divine warrior, the hunter becomes the prey.[6]

The last chapter in Nahum presents a lament concerning the fate of Nineveh. It seeks to express the tragedy over Nineveh's demise brought about by God's anger. The passage asserts that it was the Lord who defeated the great city, not the Babylonian and Median armies. The majesty of the Lord contrasts with the nothingness of human achievements. The lament calls Nineveh the "bloody city" (Nahum 3:1). The bigger a city, the harder its fall. The list of sins committed by the Assyrians included rebellion against God, idolatry, wickedness, shedding of innocent blood, lying, enslaving nations, cruelty, excessive pride, and the forced exile of people. The prophet provides a detailed description of the battle that will result in deaths without number. Even those who have survived the battle will be as good as dead.

Nahum portrays Nineveh as a shamed woman (verses 4-6) who once cleverly practiced her sorceries. Female figures commonly served as metaphors for cities in Bible times. The prophet reminds his audience that Nineveh used to seduce the nations into her alliance only to exploit them.

But now she stands disgraced by God who is her judge. Those around her treat her with contempt, and she has become a spectacle for all to watch. Shamefully exposed before the surrounding nations, she has no one to mourn her fate.

In verse 8 Nahum compares Nineveh to the Egyptian capital city of Thebes. Also known by the name of No-Amon, Thebes was one of the most impressive and wealthy cities in ancient times. In it was the great temple to the god Amon. "Are you better than Thebes?" asks the prophet. Who could answer better than Assyria who was responsible for the city's destruction? The prophet warns that in Assyria's devastation of Thebes one could see Nineveh's own ominous fate. It will drink the wine from the cup of God's anger (verse 11). The image of a cup in the Bible symbolizes destiny leading either to salvation or to judgment—as is the case here.

Nahum's book closes with two addresses, one to Nineveh (verses 12-17), and the other to its king (verses 18, 19). Speaking to the city, the prophet says that the Assyrian fortresses are like ripe figs that fall easily from a shaken tree. The empire's security has vanished, because the soldiers have lost their masculine vigor and have become "weaklings" (verse 13). The Hebrew has them as "women," the gender one did not expect to be soldiers. It is possible that Nahum builds here on the metaphor of a drunken woman implied in verse 11. Fire and sword will be the means of Nineveh's destruc-tion (verses 13-15). All preparations to prevent this from happening or for withstanding the siege will be proven fruitless. The city will be laid waste just as a swarm of locusts devastate a field, devouring whatever lies in their way. No matter the number of Nineveh's defenders or how solid the siege preparations, all of it would be to no avail.

The influential people such as merchants and court officials flee the city (verses 16, 17) while those who surround the king are sound asleep (verse 18). They offer no help during the invasion. The Lord holds the king of Assyria personally responsible for not protecting his people. He leaves them as unprotected as a flock scattered in the wilderness. The monarch should be sentenced to death for such failure. The last verse of the book reaffirms the fact that Assyria's wound is incurable. As they welcome the end of the oppressor with joy, all will recognize that the Lord is righteous. When the judgment concludes, nothing will remain of the nation most feared in ancient history.[7]

People celebrated the end of the World War II in Europe with music and dancing. Multitudes of people were happy and grateful to be alive after such a perilous period of history. The victorious Allies held many war prisoners, some of them notorious killers. A special body of experts decreed that such brutal murderers should be tried by an international code of right and wrong that applies to every person on earth. Those guilty of war crimes under such a higher law were condemned to death because of their inhumane deeds against innocent people. Thus in the end these brutal killers became victims of the same violence they had used against others. Nahum's closing message is that Nineveh's fate symbolizes the end of every oppressor on earth. The promise that God is still in charge has been a source of comfort to the faithful throughout the world's history.

[1] Historians have called Assyria the world's first great empire.

[2] S. Kealy, *An Interpretation of the Twelve Minor Prophets of the Hebrew Bible,* pp. 112, 113.

[3] The original Hebrew word, *sepher,* may be translated as either "scroll" or "book."

[4] Scholars have called the hymn a "theophoric poem."

[5] Kealy, p. 116.

[6] Francisco O. Garcia-Treto, "The Book of Nahum: Introduction, Commentary, and Reflections," *The New Interpreter's Bible* (Nashville: Abingdon Press, 1996), vol. 7, p. 612.

[7] D. Clark and J. Brunt, eds., *Introducing the Bible,* p. 305.

Chapter 8

Messages From the Book of Habakkuk

In a speech at the Brandenburg Gate in Berlin, Germany, commemorating the city's seven hundred fiftieth anniversary, United States president Ronald Reagan challenged the leader of the Soviet Union, Mikhail Gorbachev, to tear down the Berlin Wall. As an important part of the iron curtain, the wall was an image of the cold war and a symbol of tyranny. About a month after the wall had fallen, a number of famous musicians gave a concert in Berlin. It performed Beethoven's "Ode to Joy" with the word "joy" changed to "freedom." The orchestra and choir came from many countries of Europe and beyond.

Many oppressed nations had greeted the fall of Nineveh in 612 B.C. with joy and celebration. During Habakkuk's time Babylon emerged as the ancient Near East's next empire. God told the prophet that He would use Babylon's fierce soldiers to punish the sins of the kingdom of Judah. Like his contemporary Jeremiah, Habakkuk proclaimed that the Lord would use an invading foreign army as His instrument of judgment, but then in turn it would itself be judged because of its own pride and idolatry (Hab. 1:6-11; Jer. 4:13; 5:15-17; 6:22, 23; 50; 51).

The Bible tells us very little about Habakkuk beyond the prophet's name and occupation. His name was most likely non-Hebrew and is of uncertain meaning. Judging by the presence of a psalm in chapter 3, Habakkuk may have belonged to the tribe of Levi and thus served in the Temple in Jerusalem. He prophesied during the reign of King Jehoiakim of Judah (609-598) and was a contemporary of the prophets Jeremiah, Zephaniah, and Nahum.[1] The date of the revelation given to Habakkuk is clearly after the 612 B.C. destruction of the city of Nineveh. In the apocryphal story called "Bel and the Dragon" an angel prompts Habakkuk, the son of Jesus from the tribe of Levi, to bring food to the prophet Daniel who was in the lions' den.

Habakkuk is an unusual prophetic book in that it does not directly address the nation of Israel. Instead, we have a dialogue between the prophet and the Lord followed by a lament and a psalm. The questions Habakkuk raised first deal with the degeneration of his own nation. As was the case with other biblical prophets, his central concern was justice, and he predicted the demise of Judah's unjust society after the death of King Josiah. The prophet complained about the abuses coming from money lenders, the violent, drunkards, and idol worshippers. Another topic the book addresses is about living beneath a power that slays nations without pity. Can a cruel army fulfill the will of a just and righteous God? "The challenge of believing in the ultimate power of justice in a world that appears to be overwhelmingly unjust is one of the most difficult existential struggles the religious person must face."[2]

This short prophetic book of only 56 verses has a very simple outline. First we find Habakkuk's two questions and God's answers (Hab. 1; 2). Then come the "woe" speeches or laments against foreigners (Hab. 2). Finally in response to God's assurance, the prophet composed a psalm of praise at the end of which he expressed his absolute trust in God (Hab. 3). In the psalm the prophet prays for a renewal of the kind of divine redemptive activity that he had heard about in the past.[3] The book contains a rich collection of literary types, including dialogue, woe, oracle, complaint, psalm of praise, etc. A scroll found at Qumran *(Pesher Habakkuk)* is the earliest known phrase-by-phrase commentary on a biblical book.

Habakkuk's book consists of a collection of prophetic speeches with a remarkably unified theme. It addresses the problem of theodicy: the defense of the rightness of God's ways. Other parts of the Bible that deal with the issue include the whole book of Job, Psalms 37 and 73, and Jeremiah 12. Habakkuk's book opens with a prophetic call for judgment on those who had broken God's covenant with Israel. The Lord needs to take action because of His righteous and holy character. The debate between Habakkuk and God employs only general terms to designate the key actors involved so as to point to the timeless aspect of the prophetic message. Thus the word "wicked" applies in the widest sense to all unrestrained oppressors, while the word "righteous" stands for all helpless victims.

The book begins with a sigh ("How long!") and ends with a song of faith and hope in the Lord. In other words, the author's journey from doubt to faith began with a complaint, but it ended in praise and joy. So we may put the message of the book in a few simple words: Be joyful while you wait for God to intervene! Have faith, because in spite of appearances the Lord is still in charge! To the question "Is it possible to have a positive and trusting attitude in spite of adverse life situations?" the book's answer is clear: It is possible for the believer, regardless of circumstances, to live, even rejoice, without clear answers to life's problems.

Like many other authors of biblical books, Habakkuk discovers that things often get worse before they can improve. We can commend the prophet's attitude, because he took his questions directly to God in prayer. While waiting on the Lord he honestly talked to Him, and then he obediently listened. The greatness of genuine faith is that it does not depend on the fulfillment of its expectations but on its power to transform the lives of believers. The Reformer John Calvin rightly observed that Habakkuk exhorted the godly to patience by his own example.

The Dialogue With the Lord

Habakkuk is one of the three persons given the formal title "prophet" in the first verses of their books.[4] He received the revelation in a vision. The original Hebrew word for "vision" can also mean "burden," and Scripture often uses it for prophecy concerning a foreign nation (Isa. 13:1; Nahum 1:1). The prophet laments the fact that God has long delayed His justice (Hab. 1:2). But he finds courage to question the Lord, just as Gideon did long before (Judges 6:13) as well as some of the authors of biblical psalms (Ps. 3, 12, 13, 22, etc). The psalms of lament express cries to the Lord to rescue the suffering child of God and establish justice on earth. Habakkuk's first question came out of his passionate search for God's ways in the world.

The big question the prophet faced was how to relate the concept of a just God with that of an unjust world. Habakkuk lists sins of oppression such as injustice, destruction of property and people, and violence and strife (Hab. 1:3). The wicked use violence and plunder the righteous. We know that injustice, the shedding of innocent blood (Jer. 22:13-17), and the killing of prophets (Jer. 26:20-23) characterized King Jehoiakim's reign. The king even dared to burn Jeremiah's scroll (Jer. 36:22, 23). The prophet says that the basis of God's order for society is being paralyzed (Hab. 1:4). The wicked rule over the righteous while the weak find themselves victimized and can only call to God for help.

The Lord's answer to the first question consists of an announcement of judgment on Judah (verses 5-11). Since the command "Look" is in the plural, it is addressed to the whole nation. All people will gaze in amazement at the events of the judgment, so God tells the prophet to watch for it to take place. The name "Chaldean" used in verse 6 (NRSV) refers to the

Neo-Babylonian kingdom whose soldiers destroyed the Jerusalem Temple in 586 B.C. Armies in Bible times used horses and chariots for mobility and offensive power. The Babylonians, who were a law to themselves (verse 7), would lay siege to the city's fortresses. Their armies constantly overwhelm defenseless kingdoms and enslave their populations. God will use this cruel nation to punish Judah. The Lord is still in control of the world, and His hand executes justice in the world. The rise and fall of earthly kingdoms testify to this truth (cf. Dan. 2).

Babylon was a proud and arrogant nation that tried to set itself up in God's place. It spread terror and dread everywhere it went. The prophet compares the invaders' speed and might with those of the leopard, the wolf, and the eagle. The empire's armies are as devastating as the east wind that sweeps in from the desert and scorches the earth and all life on it. Their soldiers are as numerous as the sand, and no nation can resist Babylon's conquest (Hab. 1:10, 11). *Iraq*

In his second question Habakkuk raises the issue of God's mode of punishment. While the first question concerned evil at the national level, the second had to do with the international scene (verse 12). The wicked in the first lament are the corrupt aristocracy around King Jehoiakim of Judah, while those in the second lament are the Neo-Babylonians, also known as the Chaldeans. They stand in contrast with God's holy nature, which cannot tolerate evil. Israel's covenant God is eternal and just, and that is why He is called the Rock. Habakkuk's book brings together God's absolute righteousness face-to-face with the reign of seemingly unrestrained evil in the world.

Human life appears so unimportant to the conquering army that it compares its captives to the fish caught in a net and dragged to death (verses 14-16). Like fish, humans have no ruler. The bigger fish swallows the smaller. So the prophet is asking: How long will the oppressor prosper? He notices that in the real world the wicked go unpunished and the righteous unrewarded. Habakkuk casts his questions in the familiar lament form beginning with the word "How?" The prophet climbs up a tower of the city defenses in search of God's response (Hab. 2:1). He takes the position of a watchman as he waits for an answer.

In the shortest speech in the book (verses 2, 3) God tells Habakkuk to record the revelation he receives for an appointed future time. The prophet must write down the vision plainly so that once it is fulfilled its trustworthiness will be confirmed. The account must be concise enough that it can be quickly read from the tablets. In other words, Habakkuk should pre-serve the vision in such a way that a running messenger can carry it and proclaim it to the people. Although the prophetic book does not disclose the content of the message, the context of the passage makes it clear that it is a message of hope for God's people. Since according to biblical writers God Himself sets and changes "times and seasons" (Dan. 2:21), the fulfill-ment of the vision may appear slow in coming in the human timetable. Yet the possibility of an apparent delay will not take away the certainty of its fulfillment. Divine action may seem postponed, but it will certainly come to pass. The Lord Himself pledges that the vision will be fulfilled in the future (cf. Dan. 12:7; Rev. 10:5, 6). That is why the prophet should await faithfully the appointed time when God will settle injustice. The emphasis on patient waiting is typical of biblical apocalyptic literature. Jewish tradi-tion associates Habakkuk 2:2 with the coming of the Messiah. *The just shall live by faith*

Many Bible students consider Habakkuk 2:4 to be the climax of the book. A Jewish rabbi taught that it summarizes all of the commandments. The verse points out the contrast between the proud and the righteous. While death is the destiny of the arrogant, life awaits the faithful. Only a righteous and faithful person can wait for the Lord's intervention. The Hebrew noun for "faithfulness" *('emunah)* expresses a type of trust in God much deeper than the belief-centered word "faith" (2 Chron. 19:9; Isa. 7:9; Hosea 2:20). Meaning firmness or fidelity, it is a quality of God's character (Ps. 89:1, 2). In fact, faithfulness is God's gift to the righteous. Here the Lord invites the prophet to remain faithful to divine promises even when justice appears to be absent from the world.

Habakkuk 2:4 contrasts the Babylonians who are full of pride and the just people who live by faith. The verse declares that, unlike the arrogant, the just shall live because of their faithfulness to God. The apostle Paul made the second half of the verse the pillar of the biblical teaching about salvation through faith. He quotes it in Romans 1:17 and Galatians 3:11. The author of Hebrews cites Habakkuk 2:3, 4 (Heb. 10:35-38) to encourage the believ-ers of his time who endured persecution because of their faith. He applies the fulfillment of verse 3 to the second coming of Jesus Christ. And Habak-kuk 2:4 is the verse that changed the life of the great Protestant Reformer Martin Luther. Luther believed that the verse teaches that godly people were saved from destruction and lived because they waited on the Lord.

All human beings experience a tension between God's promises and events in the real world. Yet the book of Habakkuk teaches that God's power to destroy evil is absolutely reliable, because He is the Lord of impossible things. Just as Babylon destroyed many nations, so will itself perish. Evil is moving toward its predestined end. Violence will come back on violent people. The Lord may appear to be silent for a time, but not forever. Although Habakkuk did not live to see Babylon's fate, he still trusted God's promises. Faithfulness to the one whose promises never fail always characterized the prophet's life. He looked forward to the day when God's glory would fill the whole earth (verse 14).

A Lament Followed by a Praise

God's second answer to Habakkuk continues through a series of woe oracles that speak about the fall of the tyrant (verses 6-20). Five inescapable judgments will come on the unrighteous. People sometimes use the "woes" listed here as part of funeral ceremonies. In the passage the defeated nations address their conqueror directly, pointing to a reversal of its fortunes. Babylon is a negative example to others, and it serves as an object lesson of what happens to those who challenge God's plans. As it relentlessly pursued wealth, security, and fame, all of which consumed much time and energy, it forgot that such values are all transitory in character. Like death, this nation seems never satisfied in its insatiable desire for conquest and expansion. Babylon is drunk (verse 5; cf. Jer. 51:7; Dan. 5:1-7), and such intoxication will lead to ruin.

The first "woe," dealing with the excessive accumulation of wealth, addresses those who acquire goods dishonestly (Hab. 2:6-8). They rob the poor and the needy, causing them to be enslaved. Some day the victims will rise up to avenge themselves. The plunderer will be plundered, and the huge wealth of the oppressor will be reduced to poverty. The second "woe" focuses on those who search for safety while closing their ears to cries for help (verses 9-11). Such a house of avarice too will lead to destruction, and its very stones will cry out in protest at the injustice committed by its owner. The third "woe" protests bloodshed and violence (verses 12-14; cf. 3:2). The Lord of hosts has declared that Babylon's magnificent buildings will go up in smoke.

Babylon's violence will disappear while the divine kingdom will spread worldwide. The world's injustices will come to an end only through God's decisive intervention in history. After the destruction of the enemy the knowledge of the Lord will fill the earth like waters cover the sea (Hab. 2:14). The complete vindication of the righteous belongs to the reality that lies beyond the present earthly life. God calls the faithful to wait until the time that He has fully and forever intervened into human events. "The faith that strengthened Habakkuk and all the holy and the just in those days of deep trial was the same faith that sustains God's people today. In the darkest hours, under circumstances the most forbidding, the Christian believer may keep his soul stayed upon the source of all light and power. Day by day, through faith in God, his hope and courage may be renewed."[5]

The next "woe" passes judgment on Babylon's practice of intoxicating people so as to shame them (verses 15-17). Because of this, Babylon will have to drink God's cup of wrath and punishment. Its unjust pursuit of fame will result in its own humiliation. God laments the fact that Babylon sacrificed Lebanon's beautiful forests on the altar of the empire's insatiable hunger for glory. The last "woe" concerns idolatry (verses 18-20). It condemns idol worship. The Bible often associates idolatry with oppression and injustice. The oracle calls Babylon's gods *('elohim)* "worthless" *('el-ilim),* and those who put trust in them will in the end be disappointed. The Lord, on the other hand, is seated in His Temple (verse 20). His holy and majestic presence inspires awe and silence (Ps. 46:10; Isa. 41:1; Zeph. 1:7) as it extends to all the earth. Oppressors come and go, but God's presence and truth abide forever.

Habakkuk 3:1-19 presents a psalm of praise. It comes in response to God's answers to the prophet's questions. Habakkuk praises God for who He is and for His creation, and he closes with a statement of faith and trust. The first verse certifies the authenticity of the psalm as well as calling it a prayer. The Hebrew word transliterated *shigionoth* may be a musical or literary term indicating some kind of special treatment of the psalm (cf. Ps. 7). The last chapter of Habakkuk's book teaches that an adequate answer to the question of divine justice cannot be found apart from the experience of worship.

The chapter presents a theophany or a vision of God's direct appearance to save His people like when He came to Mount Sinai. The passage contains a strong affirmation of God's complete power over creation and history, and a prayer to Him to demonstrate His power by repeating His salvation acts. The book ends in unshakable confidence in God and a joyous declaration of absolute trust in the Lord. In other words, Habakkuk's is a joyful faith. The prophet stands in awe as he considers God's past deeds, His power and sovereignty (Hab. 3:2). He trusts and hopes that the Lord can repeat His mighty acts in the present. God remembers His covenant of love toward those who know Him. He is ready to forgive because of His compassions.

God's power is evident in history (verses 3-15). Heading into battle as a man of war, He rides His chariot, using His bow and sword. He employs thunderstorm and lightning as weapons. The psalm describes God's mighty acts during the Exodus and on Mount Sinai. God's two attendants, plague and pestilence, remind one of the plagues sent against the gods of Egypt (verse 5; Ex. 12:12). Hills and mountains trembled and shook when the Holy One came to Sinai. The nomad tribes from the south feel the impact of the Lord's coming (Hab. 3:7). The future "will bring the end of historical evil and the inauguration of God's cosmic reign."[6] The Lord will defeat the powers of wickedness and establish His reign on earth. The big picture about God's dealings gives us a better perspective on life and history.

Since the psalm portrays the enemy as large bodies of water, the Lord goes out as the divine warrior and confronts the mighty sea (verse 8). Horses and chariots are associated with the crossing of the Red Sea. But in this case they belong to God and bring salvation to His people against the enemy's horses and chariots. God takes His bow and His arrows that flash like lightning (verses 9-11). His presence reshapes rivers and mountains, reminding one of Creation and the great Flood. The heavenly bodies in their perpetual orbit are also affected just as they once were during the time of Joshua. Darkness symbolizes God's judgment. The Lord promises to triumph completely over hostile nations such as Babylon (verse 12).

A promise of salvation awaits those led by God's anointed servant in obedience to the terms of His covenant. Although the enemies expected a great victory, they perished because of God's intervention. They will be completely defeated, beginning with their ruler (verse 14) who will be pierced by his own spear and will not be able to take any plunder from his victims. The ones who will benefit from God's victory are the poor and the oppressed. The restless sea symbolizing the enemy now comes under His complete control (verse 15).

In a direct address to God, Habakkuk records his own reaction to the display of unlimited divine power. He responds to the Lord's intervention in history with a mixture of fear, awe, and joy (verse 16). His whole body trembles, for the revelation he is entrusted with is mostly about judgment. But soon he overcomes his fear and can talk to God and place his trust in Him. No matter how hard life might become, Habakkuk would find strength in the Lord and rejoice in Him. The prophet will wait for the day of the Lord that will bring calamity on the invading nation. Babylon's fall will be a sign of the final day of judgment on the whole world. Greed and violence will vanish when the whole world submits to the Lord's dominion.

The Lord's grace extends to His people as well as to the prophet personally (verses 17-19). In an agrarian/pastoral society people depended on crops such as barley, grapes, figs, and olives, and also on cattle raising. But the prophet claims that the Creator-God is the ultimate source of his sustenance. Though surrounded by despair, he can still rejoice because of his relationship with the Lord, something that no enemy can ever take away (cf. Rom. 8:38, 39). It has been aptly stated that in the midst of deprivation and suffering Habakkuk "still feels able to call God 'mine.'"[7] An important lesson to draw from the book's closing passage is that faithfulness should never be based on emotions only, but on the firm principles that come from a living relationship with God. Such joyful confidence gave the prophet energy to walk on heights like a deer (verse 19).

----

[1] A Jewish tradition places his ministry much earlier during the reign of King Manasseh (687-642).

[2] Theodore Hiebert, "The Book of Habakkuk: Introduction, Commentary, and Reflections," *The New Interpreter's Bible* (Nashville: Abingdon, 1996), vol. 7, p. 624.

[3] D. Clark and J. Brunt, eds., *Introducing the Bible,* p. 341.

[4] The other two are Haggai and Zechariah.

[5] Ellen G. White, *Prophets and Kings* (Mountain View, Calif.: Pacific Press Pub. Assn., 1943), p. 386.

[6] Hiebert, p. 654.

[7] David W. Baker, *Nahum, Habakkuk and Zephaniah: An Introduction and Commentary* (Downers Grove, Ill.: InterVarsity Press, 1988), p. 77.

Chapter 9

Messages From the Book of Zephaniah

The Greek philosopher Diogenes was once seen walking through the streets of Athens carrying a lamp in broad daylight. When asked what he was doing, he replied, "I am looking for an honest man." In the beginning of his book the prophet Zephaniah describes the Lord God going through the streets of Jerusalem with a lamp in His hand, seeking those who live with a sense of false security (Zeph. 1:12). An important teaching of the book is that no evildoer can escape the searching lamp of the Lord, while at the same time God will never reject any repentant sinner.

Zephaniah was a citizen of Jerusalem. His roots went back to King Hezekiah (715-687 B.C.) of Judah, an ancestor of Josiah the reformer (640-609 B.C.). The prophet's name means "the Lord shelters or protects (the just)," and it aptly summarizes a major theme of the book (Zeph. 2:3; 3:12). Zephaniah's and Jeremiah's ministries followed those of Amos, Hosea, Isaiah, and Micah. The latter prophets served about a century earlier. In fact "Zephaniah's was the first prophetic voice to be raised in Judah against its people's disobedience to God since the time of Isaiah, some seventy years earlier during Hezekiah's reign."[1] Besides Jeremiah, Zephaniah was a contemporary of Nahum and Habakkuk, all of whom ministered to the nation of Judah prior to the exile to Babylon.

Thus he prophesied either during Manasseh's reign or at the very beginning of Josiah's reform some time prior to 612 B.C. Manasseh's approach to religion was syncretistic, because it included veneration and worship of gods from different countries, especially the east. Josiah's reform gained momentum when the high priest found in the Temple a copy of the lost scroll of the Torah of Moses. John Calvin, however, placed Zephaniah's ministry after Josiah's reform, explaining that God's people were habitually unfaithful to Him. If Calvin was right, then Zephaniah's messages show that Josiah's reforms were not as radical and widespread as we might conclude from the historical books (2 Kings 23:31–24:4). But clearly Jeremiah and Zephaniah strongly supported religious reform.

The book of Zephaniah is a call to spiritual renewal as it presents God's vision of a world free from injustice, idolatry, and oppression. Zephaniah decried violence, fraud, and pride. He originally addressed his messages to Judah and the city of Jerusalem, also called Zion. But since the Lord is the sovereign of all the earth, His judgment is universal and includes the nations. It proceeds from His holy nature and from His covenant. Two dominant themes in the book are the day of the Lord and the concept of the saved remnant, a group described as humble and lowly (Zeph. 3:12). The remnant has a future of hope, because its members trust in God. The same hope is offered to the nation, as we see evident from the outline of the book. It begins with judgment against Judah, followed by oracles against foreign nations and promises of salvation and restoration. Then it ends with a message of hope and comfort for the faithful people of all times, especially the prophet's own.

The message of Zephaniah centers on the topic of the day of the Lord, one also found in other prophetic books (cf. Isa. 2; 13; 34; Jer. 46; Eze. 7; Joel 2; Amos 5). Like a two-sided coin, the day of the Lord will bring both judgment and salvation. Sins such as idolatry and pride precipitate its coming. The day of the Lord will be a time of anger, distress, anguish, ruin, devastation, darkness, trumpet blast, and battle. Martin Luther stated that the gospel as presented in Zephaniah is an outpouring of God's anger that calls for true repentance. The book combines threats of universal judgment with ringing promises of a worldwide restoration. The only direct New Testament reference to Zephaniah is the phrase the "great day of God the Almighty" found in the book of Revelation (Rev. 16:14).

Zephaniah's opening verse states that God commissioned the prophet to speak to the people of Judah during the reign of Josiah (Zeph. 1:1). Josiah became king at the age of 8 after the assassination of his father, Amon, in a palace coup (2 Kings 21; 22). The son's reform went through a serious setback because of Josiah's untimely death at the battle of Haran in 609 B.C. The prophet calls his book "the word of the Lord," a designation used by many other prophets in the Bible.[2] Although he was the son of Cushi, Zephaniah's family worshiped the true God. The name Cushi is either a proper name or an ethnic designation that suggests an African ancestry (cf. Num. 12:1; 2 Sam. 18:21; Jer. 36:14). Ancient Egyptian texts use "Kush" to refer to the region of the Upper Nile called Nubia. One of Zephaniah's oracles against foreign nations addresses the Cushites (Zeph. 2:12).

Warning of a Coming Destruction

Zephaniah's book opens with a dramatic imagery of God sweeping the creation clean (Zeph. 1:2). The judgment is universal, an undoing of God's creation. But it will focus especially on the human race. Such worldwide destruction reminds one of the great Flood (Gen. 6; 7). The words "sweep away" point to its finality (cf. Jer. 4:23-26). The prophet then concentrates on the nation of Judah (Zeph. 1:4). "The sin of Judah has affected the cosmos to its very created roots."[3] God will punish Jerusalem based on the terms of His covenant with it.

The prophet most likely delivered his first message during the Feast of Tabernacles, which commemorated God's care and protection over Israel in the wilderness. Only this time God's hand, which symbolizes power, would go against His people. The two specific charges brought up against Judah are idolatry and indifference toward God. Zephaniah speaks against the people who worship Baal, the Canaanite storm god, and follow his priests. Even in the early phase of Josiah's reform a "remnant of Baal" still remained in the land. The prophet speaks of the worship of astral deities from the roofs, a practice especially common in Mesopotamia (verse 5). Thus the people of Judah mixed the worship of the Lord with other deities and swore by the names of many idols. They treated the Lord as someone who no longer existed and could offer no guidance and hope.

The prophet tells his listeners to be silent and place their hope in the presence of the sovereign Lord (verse 7; cf. Hab. 2:20). An attitude of silence evokes awe and respect, and it also indicates the nearness of the day of the Lord. Zephaniah symbolizes the judgment by a sacred feast during which the Lord appears as a high priest. God then offers a special sacrifice. Sinners are the offering, and enemy invaders are the invited guests. A part of this consecration is the punishment of high-ranking officials and princes (Zeph. 1:8). Belonging to the royal line, they wear foreign clothes that may have been used for pagan religious customs (cf. 2 Kings 10:22).[4] These same leaders practice violence and deceit instead of justice and righteousness.

Faced with the prospect of a great destruction, Jerusalem's population will wail in anguish. The cries of distress come from the northern side of Jerusalem where the city is especially vulnerable to enemy attacks (Zeph.

1:10, 11). The first persons to be wiped out will be the merchants in the marketplace who deal dishonestly with their customers. (Pieces of silver served as currency before the introduction of coinage.) God will search the city with lamps so that no sinner may escape (verse 12; cf. Eze. 9). The word "lamps" is in the plural, suggesting that God and the invading armies join together on the search mission. No one will be able to hide.

The condemnation will also fall on the complacent wicked persons whom the prophet compares to wine that has sat too long and become spoiled. The same fate will strike the rich who oppress the poor. The unjust wealth of those who own houses and vineyards will be confiscated. People have slipped into such apathy that they consider God completely detached and uninvolved in history and human society. Yet the Bible repeatedly describes God as someone constantly active in the lives of both individuals and the nations, and especially in the history of His people. Zephaniah quotes some of his contemporaries as saying that the Lord will do nothing either good or bad. Such a distorted view of God has some serious consequences. It is sometimes better to see God acting and argue against it, than not to see Him involved at all.

Zephaniah then presents one of the greatest portrayals of judgment in the Bible (Zeph. 1:14). It consists of a detailed description of the day of the Lord that the prophet declares is near. We should understand the word "near" qualitatively as "certain" or "sure" and not only quantitatively meaning "near in time." A warrior announces the day through a battle cry. Divine wrath results in human anguish and destruction and also in devastation of nature. Deep darkness and gloom enhance terror. The trumpet blast and battle cry connote a war situation. The city's towers and fortresses will not protect anyone from the coming judgment. "Clearly, the great day of the Lord, a day of distress, devastation, and darkness was to be all-encompassing."[5]

The sixfold use of the word "day" in Zephaniah 1:15, 16, an echo of Creation week, confirms the fact that the events on the day of the Lord represent a reversal of God's creation. The Lord pronounces His judgment on all humankind that sinned against Him. The precious blood that symbolizes life will be as cheap as the dust of the ground. Neither wealth (silver and gold) nor idols will be able to save anyone from the coming wrath. The prophet compares God's zeal to fire that devours the whole world. The suddenness of misfortune (verse 18) results from the fact that it would take place at midday. No person can use a bribe as a means of escaping a judgment that like unquenchable fire will devour the whole earth.

Speaking on the subject of readiness for divine judgment, Zephaniah addresses God's people who because of the sins of idolatry have become like any other nation of the world. Two key words in Zephaniah 2:2, 3 are "before" and "seek," and each appears three times. *Before* the fierce anger of the Lord comes, the people are urged to *seek* the Lord's righteousness and humility. The word "seek" implies an active way of waiting on the Lord.

Zephaniah's call to seek justice and humility from the Lord God echoes the spirit of Micah (Micah 6:8) and Amos (Amos 5:24). The prophet delivers a message of hope to the humble of the land who rely on God because they realize their helplessness. They remain faithful to the Lord and obedient to His revealed instruction. He is their only protection on the day of wrath. Like other biblical prophets, Zephaniah taught that we should never take God's grace for granted. That is why he said, "Perhaps you will be sheltered on the day of the Lord's anger" (Zeph. 2:3; cf. Ex. 32:30; Amos 5:15; Jer. 20:10). The word "perhaps" points to God's absolute freedom to save and restore repentant sinners by His grace alone.

A Worldwide Judgment

The prophet now delivers oracles against neighboring nations (Zeph. 2:4-15). The use of the word "woe" implies a lament over the condemned people whom He has warned that destruction is coming. Indeed, the prophet's emotional reaction to the bad news ranges from anger to lament. Based on Israel's realization that their God was Lord of all nations, he holds them responsible for what they do. God's universal and natural law of justice is at work everywhere so whoever violates it will face punishment. Since the divine word concerned all peoples, the day of the Lord will have both positive and negative consequences for the nations of the world. To some it will bring doom, while to others salvation. The oracles address nations located in every direction: west, east, south, and north. Other prophets had delivered similar oracles against foreign nations (Amos 1; 2; Isa. 13-23; Jer. 46-51; Eze. 25-32).

The people of the Kerethite tribe (from Crete) of the Philistines are the object of a "woe" oracle (Zeph. 2:5). It warns four of their cities of impending destruction. The punishment on the Philistine cities should motivate the people of Judah to reform their ways. Just as the day of the Lord brings both judgment and mercy, so the concept of the remnant of the people also has a two-sided nature. It testifies not only to the loss of a nation, but also to the hope that such loss will not be total. "Destruction will come, but not annihilation."[6] The remnant of God's people will inhabit the former Philistine land when their fortunes are restored (verses 6, 7).

The next message concerns Judah's relatives, the people of Moab and Ammon (verses 8-11), who descended from the two sons of Abram's nephew, Lot. They had wronged God's people through verbal abuse and threats. The Lord of hosts will deal with them as He did with the cities of the plain near the Dead Sea. Their homeland will become ruins and salt pits. The formerly oppressed remnant of Judah will then plunder their oppressor.[7]

Zephaniah next talks against Cush (verse 12), a term that may be a general reference to Egypt. A Cushite dynasty had ruled there until Assyria's capture of Thebes. Egypt was Judah's major enemy in the south, and the Lord now warns that He will destroy its people. Assyria will suffer the same fate (verses 13-15). Its capital city Nineveh would become a desolate wilderness. Assyria came from the direction of the north, the traditional route of invading armies. Its destruction will include the animal world, reversing the closing statement from Jonah's book (Jonah 4:11).

Nineveh's most splendid buildings will become lairs for wild animals and screech owls. Various desert birds will make their nests on the pillars that still stand. "The area which for some three centuries had been the proud centre of the world would become a desert and a wasteland and would remain like this for centuries (Zeph. 2:13-15)."[8] Appalled, those who pass by can only shake their heads. Such a great city has become nothing more than the habitat of beasts. The oracle uses verbs in the past tense (prophetic perfect) to point to the certainty of the predictions. The enemy's arrogant pride has led to its downfall. Self-sufficiency usually creates a feeling of independence from God. The judgment on Nineveh will be welcome news to the oppressed people of God.

The last part of chapter 2 describes the sins of Nineveh. Since Zephaniah did not identify the city mentioned in the beginning of chapter 3, his audience thought that he was still talking about Nineveh, not realizing that the prophet had switched to the judgment on Jerusalem. He presents a lament over its unfaithfulness and rebellion. Thus the sixth and the last "woe" is against Jerusalem and its greedy leaders. The people of Judah have been disobedient and have rejected their God whom they trust no longer. Zephaniah calls corrupt officials "roaring lions" and "evening wolves." Like ferocious beasts they wait to attack their prey (cf. Ps. 22:12). They devour the flock instead of protecting them. Furthermore, they speak not God's will but lying words. The priests profane God's holy things in the sanctuary and pervert divine teaching, leading people astray. "The corruption of the city results directly from its leaders' failure to live up to their designated roles and responsibilities."⁹

But the Lord and His justice are within the city. In contrast to the corrupt leaders, He is righteous and faithful. He is still committed to His people. His presence in the city is evident because He renders judgment morning after morning (Zeph. 3:5). In Bible times the people expected justice to be dispensed at the city gates beginning with the morning hours. God Himself will see to it that the oppressed receive justice. His presence is as dependable as the sunrise. The only hope of survival is in getting rid of false pride and waiting upon the Lord.

The Lord's punishment on the nations should serve as a warning to the people of Judah. Those who did not recognize Him as Lord would face discipline. God addresses Jerusalem directly in first-person speech, warning them about the coming destruction. As the center of worship of the Lord, the city needs correction and obedience in order to avoid extinction. The prophet calls the people to accept discipline and learn from the experience of others as well as from their own (verse 7). A period of waiting still remains before God brings all nations together to render justice and to put an end to sin.

A Global Restoration

Even though fire will be the instrument of the universal judgment, its purpose is purification and healing rather than annihilation and death. In the end God will claim His righteous remnant whose tongue and lips will be purified (cf. Isa. 6). His promise of hope that He will change speech among the nations reverses the confusion of tongues after the Flood (Gen. 11:9). Zephaniah says that people will praise God with changed hearts, pure speech, and in unity. They will proclaim the Lord's name everywhere. The Lord will offer His salvation to all who agree to worship Him in accordance with the promises made to Abram (Gen. 12:1-3). The prophet portrays the Lord, His people, and the nations as all in joyful unity. They will be free from wrong, deceit, falsehood, and fear.

African nations will bring an offering to the Lord along with many others, and He will call them "mine" (Zeph. 3:10). God had originally intended that His people should be a light to the nations—even to the people in distant Africa. Perhaps we have here an allusion to Zephaniah's African ancestry. While Jerusalem's purification will be the result of God's action, unrepentant sinners will not be able to stand on God's holy hill. In the end He will triumph over foreign gods and their armies, exposing their weakness. At that time idol worshippers will turn to the true God. They will flock to Jerusalem to experience universal worship of the Lord. As for the purified remnant, they will survive the destruction because its members remained faithful to God's covenant. Truthful and humble, they trust God. As a result, they are the object of God's saving grace. The prophet presents a call to Jerusalem to rejoice (cf. Isa. 62:5; 65:19).

The concluding victory psalm shows how God also will exalt over His flock. The death sentence has been lifted, and He stands proclaimed as great King. As victorious ruler He too celebrates in the midst of His redeemed people just as David did before the ark of the Lord (2 Sam. 6:12-15). The Lord delights in His people who are invited to sing and shout because they are saved from their enemies. The Lord their king is in their midst, and they need not fear. Like a wounded lover or rejected parent reunited with their beloved, the Lord will burst into joy. He will pour abundant blessings on His people and renew them in His love. They will celebrate the love of God through their festivals (Zeph. 3:17, 18).

Zephaniah's book closes with divine promises of comfort, restoration, and hope in the Lord (verses 19, 20). Sounds of praise will fill the land in response to the people's return. The world made new will learn to worship God. Zephaniah's book began with gloom, but it ends with an ecstatic song of joy. "Life under God's reign [is described as] pastoral serenity."[10] The divine shepherd gives special care to the physically disabled and the outcast. Whereas before they were a byword of shame, now they will be praised and honored. The fortunes of God's people will be fully restored and the time of captivity will be forgotten.

Martin Luther believed that among the minor prophets, Zephaniah makes the clearest prophecies about Christ's kingdom. As Christians, we believe that it was inaugurated when Jesus Christ came down to earth and will be consummated at His return. Jesus said that a woman giving birth to a child has pain because her time has come; but when her baby is born she forgets the anguish because of her joy at its birth (John 16:21). Such hope lived in the heart of an elderly woman who for years faithfully served the Lord in the church and in her community. Every time someone asked her the question "How are you, sister?" she would always respond in the same way: "Grateful!" What an inspiration her answer is to all of us to have a positive attitude in life.

[1] Robert A. Bennet, "The Book of Zephaniah: Introduction, Commentary, and Reflections," *The New Interpreter's Bible* (Nashville: Abingdon, 1996), vol. 7, p. 661.

[2] For example, Jer. 1:2; Eze. 1:3; Hosea 1:1; Joel 1:1; Micah 1:1; Haggai 1:1; Zech. 1:1; Mal. 1:1.

[3] D. Clark and J. Brunt, eds., *Introducing the Bible,* p. 314.

[4] D. Baker, *Nahum, Habakkuk and Zephaniah,* p. 95.

[5] Clark and Brunt, p. 312.

[6] Baker, p. 106.

[7] Genesis 19 links the destruction of Sodom and Gomorrah with the story of the birth of Lot's sons.

[8] S. Kealy, *An Interpretation of the Twelve Minor Prophets of the Hebrew Bible,* p. 168.

[9] Bennet, p. 693.

[10] *Ibid.,* p. 667.

Chapter 10

Messages From the Book of Haggai

Some years ago in the country of Chile a group of 33 miners became trapped underground for more than two months. The accident happened when a rockfall caused a tunnel to collapse. With the help of a specially made capsule, rescuers winched each miner to the surface amid scenes of jubilation. Their loved ones waited at the top of the shaft to greet them. Cheers welcomed their arrival to the surface not only in the country of Chile, but around the world. United States president Barack Obama, for example, called the rescue a "tremendously inspirational story." All of the miners ascribed their survival to the providence of God to whom they had offered many fervent prayers. To family members and crowds of other people, the lives of the miners were the tangible signs of God's saving grace.

The great joy that came from the rescue of these miners reminds the readers of the Bible of the return of the remnant of Judah from their captivity in Babylon: "When the Lord brought back the captive ones of Zion, we were like those who dream. Then our mouth was filled with laughter and our tongue with joyful shouting" (Ps. 126:1, 2, NASB). The prophet Isaiah had promised about two centuries earlier that the desert would burst into flowers to greet those who returned from Babylon (Isa. 35:1, 2). "Optimism certainly must have characterized the early days of return and the initial stages of restoration."[1] The main purpose of the return from exile was the rebuilding of the Temple in Jerusalem (Ezra 1:5), the same purpose for which God had led Israel out of Egypt (Ex. 7:16; 15:17).

The realities surrounding those who returned to Palestine, however, were different, because they faced hostile neighbors, the ruins of the Temple, drought, food shortage, and poverty. "Disillusionment had set in after the first exhilarating sense of adventure had passed."[2] By the time of the prophet Haggai nearly 20 years had passed since the first group of exiles left Babylon thanks to the decree by King Cyrus of Persia. The land of Judah belonged to the fifth satrapy in the Medo-Persian Empire, the province called "Beyond the River" (Euphrates). The city of Samaria was its administrative center, because Jerusalem still lay in ruins.

The name Haggai means "festal" and usually went to a child born on a festival. The prophet's family name may have been omitted intentionally in order to focus attention on the fact that the book is primarily God's Word. The same is true of the books authored by some other prophets such as Amos, Habakkuk, and Obadiah whose family names also do not appear in the text. In other words, Haggai wanted to center attention on the message rather than on the messenger. His book five times calls him "the prophet" (1:1, 3, 12; 2:1, 10). His prophetic ministry resulted in an immediate and effective response by the people, and it parallels the successes of Jonah and Joel. Inspired by God, Haggai spoke confidently to the leaders and the people not against sins but against a lack of action. His main concern was the rebuilding of the Temple, the center of religious and community life. The Lord's presence there would bring many blessings. The new Temple would eventually be greater than the old one.

Haggai and the prophet Zechariah, his close companion, both ministered "at the same time and toward the same goal."[3] The two men were involved in the restoration of the nation of Judah and are mentioned in the book of Ezra: "Now Haggai the prophet and Zechariah the prophet, a descendant of Iddo, prophesied to the Jews in Judah and Jerusalem in the name of the God of Israel, who was over them" (Ezra 5:1; cf. 6:14). Haggai prophesied in Palestine for only a few months at the end of 520 B.C. Like Zechariah, he gives precise dates for his messages. The date of Haggai's book is one of the most certain among biblical writings.

Haggai is the second-shortest Old Testament book (after Obadiah). Its 38 verses comprise just two chapters. A narrative style dominates, and it is difficult to separate poetry from the narrative sections. The book contains a powerful message intended to lead people from apparent failure to glory. It concerned both the present and the future: The present had to do with rebuilding the Temple, while the future involved the reign of God on earth. Haggai begins his book with a call to restore the Temple (Haggai 1:1-11). Judah's difficult economic situation, he reasons, is not an excuse but the result of neglecting the Temple. The focal point of God's presence on earth should be reconstructed now. Thus one can say that Haggai was a messenger of restoration. We can summarize the theme of his book by the following three statements: "Give careful thought" (Haggai 1:5, 7; 2:15, 18). "Be strong . . . and work" (Haggai 2:4). "I am with you" (Haggai 1:13; 2:4).

Two great leaders of the Reformation, Luther and Calvin, both maintained that Haggai's prophecies, especially at the end of the book, are messianic. The goal of history is that God's kingdom should spread among all nations.

Now Is the Time!

The introductory verse to the book lists the political and spiritual leaders of Judah during Haggai's prophetic ministry. Darius I was the king of the Persian Empire, Zerubbabel was the governor, while Joshua was the high priest. Zerubbabel, grandson of Jehoiachin, a king of Judah from David's line, found himself taken captive to Babylon at a young age. The name Zerubbabel means "seed or shoot from Babylon." The Persian king made him governor of Judah. Joshua's Hebrew name means "the Lord saves."[4] He was a descendant of Zadok the high priest in the time of King David. Both men came back from Babylon and were leaders of the first group returning from exile (Ezra 3). The "first day of the month" according to the lunar calendar was the day celebrating the new moon (see Isa. 1:13; Hosea 2:11; Amos 8:5).

The words from Haggai 1:2 mark the first authentic voice of prophecy after Judah's return from captivity. Haggai, together with Zechariah, was God's voice to the people, like Moses was at the beginning of their history. The "Lord Almighty" or "Lord of hosts" (NRSV) was the title of the God who protected His people and fought in their battles. He is the Almighty God of all the earth, the Ruler of all kingdoms (verse 11). Revelation 12:7 identifies Michael as the leader of the Lord's armies, and Daniel 12:1 describes the same being as the prince protector of God's people. Since Michael at the head of the divine forces defeated Satan, we should identify Him with Jesus Christ.

The Temple in Jerusalem was the visible sign of God's abiding presence on earth. Prior to its destruction, the building was the vibrant religious, administrative, and economic heart of the nation. Through His prophet God says that the people have mistaken their priorities and failed to put Him first. They seem to have forgotten the reason of their return. Although they had rebuilt their own houses, the house of the Lord was still in ruins. Moreover, the farming work in the fields competed with the reconstruction of the Temple. For this reason God challenges the people's priorities (Haggai 1:3, 4). Their "paneled houses" stand in sharp contrast to the ruined Temple. The difference was not in the quality of the building material but rather in the state of completion.

Speaking through Haggai, God says that rising prices and inflation are

His ways of calling people to put first things first. The prophet uses the language of the covenantal blessings and curses from the books of Moses (verse 6). Since blessings such as crops, silver, and gold are God's gifts, their shortage is a sign of His displeasure. After all, God is also the provider of rain and dew (verses 9-11). So Haggai invites his audience to give careful thought to the matter. According to the original Hebrew text the prophet said: "Set your hearts on this!" (verses 5, 7). In Bible times people regarded the heart as the organ of thinking. Haggai is inviting people to action: "Act, now! Go to the mountains, get timber and build!" This, he said, will honor God who will take pleasure in such work. Haggai's zeal for the Temple reminds one of King David who said that he would not rest until he found a dwelling place for his God (Ps. 132:1-5). The preexilic prophets stressed the substance of religion over religious form, while postexilic prophets showed that religious substance needs to be expressed in the forms.

All the work on the Lord's house was done on a voluntary basis for God's pleasure and glory. The leaders and the people obeyed the Lord's Word and showed respect for Him. The architects needed timber because they placed layers of wood in the stone walls to minimize earthquake damage (Haggai 1:8). God's Spirit (verses 12, 14) moved the hearts of the community so that the people obeyed (literally "heard") the divine message under the leadership of Zerubbabel and Joshua. The verb to "hear" in the Bible is not a neutral term, but a command that requires a response of obedience (Deut. 6:4-9). Thus the remnant exchanged indifference for action. In about five years they completed the main task of rebuilding. Haggai was God's mouthpiece and His direct messenger. With the help of the Spirit the prophetic message stirred people's hearts and moved them to work. The original Hebrew employs the same word for "message" (Haggai 1:13) and for "work" (verse 14).[5] The divine message needed to be applied through work. God's words "I am with you" express the greatest promise in the Bible. It is one of protection and support.

The community resumed the rebuilding as soon as they completed urgent tasks in the fields and orchards (see verse 15). Those who began on the Temple soon needed encouragement. The second chapter contains words of comfort and promise. About a month after the project started, the Lord spoke through Haggai again to the leaders and the people (Haggai 2:1, 2). The dating of this message corresponds to the seventh day of the Feast of Tabernacles, a major religious festival that celebrated God's care for His people.

In comparison with the glory and splendor of Solomon's Temple, many members of the remnant feared that the new Temple could never match the old (verse 3). It threatened to undermine the people's energy. Haggai called the people to have confidence in what God would do in the future. The Lord was still in their midst, guaranteeing their safety. Dedication to the present task must replace nostalgia for past times. They need not fear. Calls to be brave and strong (verses 4, 5) echo those elsewhere in Scripture (cf. Deut. 31:7; Joshua 1:6, 7; 10:25; Mark 6:50), showing that God's presence gives courage and strength. Through His Spirit, God abides always with His people just as He did at the time they left Egypt and entered the land of promise.

Desire of Nations

The prophetic words concerned the future of both God's people and the nations of the world. God promises to shake all creation (Haggai 2:6, 7). While it would involve a change in the present order of things in the world, it was very different from what the king of Babylon did when he made nations shake and earth tremble (Isa. 14:16, 17). In God's appointed time the nations will obey His voice and bring their gifts to fill the Temple with splendor. Their treasures will glorify the new Temple, making it special in God's eyes. The original Hebrew expression describing the precious gifts that the nations would supply the new Temple may also be translated as "the desire of all nations."

The Hebrew word for "desire" describes precious and desirable things (cf. Ezra 8:27). The Latin Vulgate applied the word "desire" to the Messiah. John Calvin affirmed that Christ is the treasure of all nations. The primary reason for which the new Temple's glory would exceed the previous one is that the Messiah, the One greater than the Temple (Matt. 12:6), would enter it. Haggai also declares that the Lord is the ultimate owner of gold and silver (Haggai 2:8). But God's concern went beyond the Temple. He wanted to bless the people not only spiritually but also with material blessings. The New Testament shows how the Messiah brought peace and other blessings to the human race aptly expressed in the word "shalom" (Matt. 11:28-30), one rich in meanings.

About two months later Haggai received a new message from God (Haggai 2:10). Concerned with issues of holiness and defilement, it addressed the priests who were entrusted with the divine teaching called the Torah of Moses. Just as the sacrifice for sin known as "the sin offering" was most holy, so the priests' robes were considered holy. Yet while ritual defilement was always contagious, holiness was not. In other words, there is a limit to the extent to which holiness is transferable, whereas contamination by uncleanness goes much further. The conclusion is that priestly holiness, no matter how great it might be, could not overcome the people's uncleanness.

Haggai applied this conclusion to the present situation. The altar in the Temple needed to be consecrated from the previous defilements so that sacrifices would be accepted by the Lord. Although God's people comprised a holy nation, they had contaminated everything they came in contact with through their sins. The impurity in this case had to do with the failure to take seriously the work on God's Temple.

A specially appointed day would mark the beginning of a renewal of the relationship between God and the community. Outside of God's healing power, there is no remedy to sin. In the past He had readily punished His people for their indifference. But on the day the foundation stone of the Lord's Temple was laid and the Temple was rededicated, a new era of prosperity would begin. "From this day on I will bless you," God said (verse 19). The newly sown seed would yield an abundant harvest. The Gospel writers quoted Jesus' claim that He is the cornerstone and the foundation of a new temple that is His church.

For a second time God says that He will shake the heaven and the earth (verse 21). The same Lord who controls the movements of Planet Earth also works through people. The mighty convulsions would result in the restoration of David's royal line. God had chosen Zerubbabel from David's line to honor in a special way. The Lord would work in behalf of His people through Zerubbabel's descendant whom the prophets called the Lord's "chosen servant" (cf. Isa. 40-55). That is most likely the reason why Scripture never refers to Zerubbabel as king while Haggai introduces Darius as king in the first verse of the book.

Like his ancestor David, Zerubbabel has been selected by God to be His "servant." He is the signet ring (Haggai 2:23) entrusted with power and authority.[6] The Lord employs the expression "signet ring" in relation to Shealtiel, son of Jehoiachin, Judah's king whom the Babylonians had taken into exile. Zerubbabel was to be the new signet ring on the Lord's hand. Yet he is the signet ring, not the king! In the genealogies of the Gospels Zerubbabel serves as an important link between David and David's Son, Jesus the Messiah (Matt. 1:12; Luke 3:27).

The Lord pledges to lead His people into the future. The power of Israel's God extends even beyond the borders of Judah. As the Creator-God, He is capable of shaking the earth's foundation and establishing a new order among the nations of the world. Armed with this kind of revelation, God's people should take courage and work with their whole heart to make God's house glorious so as to welcome the coming of the great King. While resisting discouragement, each generation should "take courage in God's goodness and to work on behalf of God's purposes."[7]

---

[1] D. Clark and J. Brunt, eds., *Interpreting the Bible*, p. 383.

[2] Joyce G. Baldwin, *Haggai, Zechariah, and Malachi: An Introduction and Commentary* (Downers Grove, Ill.: InterVarsity Press, 1972), p. 37.

[3] Eugene March, "The Book of Haggai: Introduction, Commentary, and Reflections," *The New Interpreter's Bible* (Nashville: Abingdon Press, 1996), vol. 7, p. 708.

[4] The name in Aramaic is *Yeshua*, like the name of Jesus.

[5] The Hebrew word *mel'akah* is also related to the noun *mal'ak* from verse 13.

[6] S. Kealy, *An Interpretation of the Twelve Minor Prophets of the Hebrew Bible*, p. 183.

[7] March, p. 725.

Chapter 11

Messages From the Book of Zechariah

The book *A Promise Kept*[1] tells a compelling true story of love and devotion. Robertson, a distinguished man in Christian academic circles, is shocked when his wife, Muriel, is diagnosed with Alzheimer's disease. Gradually she succumbs to its ravages. As the disease takes its toll on Muriel, Robertson devotes more and more time to watching over her. He leaves his work and other pursuits to care for his ill wife, because without his presence, she is fearful and agitated. Only with him near is she happy and content. Eventually she becomes totally dependent upon him, unable to perform rudimentary tasks or even converse. The heart of the story is that he remains with her gratefully, and with a loving attitude. Although he is not thrilled to watch his lovely, intelligent wife slide into helpless dementia, he sees his caretaking as a holy task, one entrusted to him by God. Robertson remembers his wedding promise to Muriel to the end.

The name Zechariah means "the Lord remembers,"[2] and it fits well the message given through the prophet. The first half of his book shows that God remembers His people and is at work in their behalf, while the second half teaches that the Lord will remember them at the time of the end and deliver them from their enemies. The historical setting of Zechariah's ministry is the same as that of Haggai. The book of Ezra always mentions the two names together.[3] Both prophets encouraged the people to complete the work of rebuilding the Temple. Zechariah, son of Berechiah and grandson of Iddo,[4] belonged to the tribe of Levi. Iddo returned to Judea with the first group of exiles. As for Zechariah, he was a priest and head of the family (Neh.12:4, 16), but God also called him to be a prophet (Zech. 1:1). An interpreting angel acts as Zechariah's guide so that in his visions he is not a mere observer but one who takes an active role in its words and deeds.

A vital principle in interpreting a biblical book is to realize that it expresses its message not only in words but also in literary forms and structures.[5] The general plan of Zechariah's book follows a progression from the known to the unknown. An introductory call to repentance (Zech. 1:1-6) introduces a series of eight visions (Zech. 1:7-6:15). Then there are two chapters on the topic of fasting (Zech. 7; 8) followed by more apocalyptic visions (Zech. 9-14) that greatly influenced John the revelator. The closing verses in the book look forward to the time when all people will worship the true God. Thus Zechariah's visions disclose God's plan for the glorious future of Judah and other nations.

The early church translator Jerome wrote that this longest book of the minor prophets is also the most obscure, while a modern scholar has described Zechariah as "a paradoxical and enigmatic book."[6] Yet since ancient times readers have found in Zechariah numerous references to messianic times eclipsed only in number by Isaiah. The book as a whole shows a strong orientation toward the ideal future of earth's history. It is one of the most quoted and alluded Old Testament books in the New Testament because it reveals God's eternal purpose for His people and their land. God's words are gracious and comforting (Zech. 1:13), calling people to repent. His end-time intervention will halt the triumph of evil over good and establish His kingdom over all the earth.

Visions of Divine Presence

In the first verse in Zechariah's book the title "prophet" follows the author's personal name to lend the authority to the message (cf. Hab. 1:1; Haggai 1:1). The opening passage contains a brief sermon that prefaces the eight visions. It is a call to repentance and confession of the nation's evil ways. In the Bible to "repent" means to "return" to the Lord who is the covenant God and reestablish a personal relationship with Him (cf. Mal. 3:7). Divine anger, God's natural reaction to sin, led to Judah's destruction and exile. The words spoken by the prophets are God's enduring words. When obeyed, they result in blessings, but when disobeyed, they bring curses. The prophet said that it was time for renewal and spiritual restoration.

Zechariah's first vision comes at night (Zech. 1:8). The scene likely takes place in the Kidron Valley among fragrant evergreen trees, although the luxuriant shape of myrtles is suggestive of the Garden of Eden. Two heavenly messengers are present, one the Messenger of the Lord riding on a red horse, the other an interpreting angel (cf. Dan. 10). The patrolling horses report to the Lord's Messenger, who is their commander. They symbolize military power and dominion. Here the Lord has sent them on a global mission, and they announce that the earth is at peace.

For 70 years the land of Judah has lain desolate (Zech. 1:12).[7] The time is ripe to trumpet a message—that God is active and in control of history. He is zealous for His people while angry at the proud nations that oppressed them. The wrath toward His people was only temporary, so now He seeks to console Zion. God's love is intense, never passive. He announces His return to the Temple to bring comfort to the land (verse 16). "Moral transformation is not the condition of God's return, but results from it."[8] Not only the Temple but the city will be rebuilt, and the promise of restoration extends to the other cities of Judah. Divine favor and blessings will overflow from Jerusalem, bringing prosperity into the neighboring cities. Jerusalem is again the center of God's attention and activity.[9] The Lord manifests His presence in the Temple.

In his second vision (verses 18-21) Zechariah lifts up his eyes and sees four horns. A horn symbolizes strength, while the number four stands for the totality of the earth, all the directions in which the people scattered into exile. The prophet learns that the enemies that God's people most feared in past times will be overthrown and reduced to impotence, an implication clear from the picture of the four smiths who will not destroy the nations but only cut off their horns.

The third vision concerns Jerusalem (Zech. 2:1-13). While it will be a fortified city, at the same time it will be open to receive a great number of people and animals. The extraordinary increase in Jerusalem's population will make walls impossible. Its safety, though, is guaranteed, because a supernatural wall of fire will protect it from enemies. Fire in Scripture represents divine presence. Zechariah sends an open invitation to those still in exile to return and join the work of rebuilding (verse 6). He urges Zion's children to leave Babylon, because Jerusalem is the center of God's attention. He keeps His own as the apple of his eyes (cf. Deut. 32:10). Former captives will inherit the plunder of their oppressors. When these words come to pass, all will know that Zechariah spoke the truth.

God will come out of His holy dwelling in heaven. Daughter Zion will sing and rejoice, because the Lord will dwell in her midst (Zech. 2:10). The threat against Daughter Babylon is contrasted with the joy of Daughter Zion. Many nations will join themselves to the God who dwells in Zion and become His people.[10] They will all see the Lord's return and come to acknowledge Him and be part of the universal kingdom. God will call them "my people." Their inclusion, not destruction, is in view. Experiencing God's power, they will enter into a covenant with Him. The presence of the Temple will consecrate the land to make it "holy land." Awe and silence are proper responses to God's way of acting (cf. Hab. 2:20).

The setting of the visions now moves into the Temple itself. The interpreting angel shows Zechariah the heavenly courtroom where Joshua the high priest stands before the Lord's Messenger (Zech. 3:1). The adversary challenges Joshua's fitness to be high priest. As in several other passages of the Bible, the distinction between the Lord and the Messenger of the Lord blurs (cf. Gen. 22:10-15; Ex. 3:1-5). In accordance with the Lord's word that cannot be revoked, the faithful remnant represented by Joshua has been snatched from the destructive fire. "Joshua in his high-priestly role stood for the predicament of the whole people, who had incurred the divine wrath, suffered the penalty of the exile, and now knew that they needed a way back to the presence of a holy God."[11]

Sins and iniquities have made the priestly garments filthy, so Joshua is unable to defend himself. To his surprise he finds his clothes suddenly changed. The removal of filthy garments represents the taking away of sins and the gift of divine acceptance (cf. Isa. 6:1-7). The new garments are suitable for the court in heaven. What is remarkable about this vision is that it depicts the granting of forgiveness of sin without the use of an animal sacrifice. The Messenger of the Lord commissions Joshua to walk in God's ways and perform faithfully his priestly duties, a commitment that will lead to special privileges such as access to God's council.

Zechariah then speaks to Joshua and the company of priests and describes them as signs of the coming servant of the Lord (Zech. 3:8). God promises to engrave a text on a commemorative stone that symbolizes the power given to a ruler.[12] The stone has seven eyes or fountains of water that will wash away sins and bring prosperity in the time to come. Characterized by peace and great blessings, that future day will be as ideal as the golden time under David and Solomon. People will socialize with their neighbors under the vine and the fig trees.

The golden lampstand, known as the menorah, stood in the holy place of the sanctuary. It was shaped as a tree trunk. In his vision Zechariah saw a bowl on its top and seven small bowls with a place for wicks (Zech. 4:1, 2). On the two sides of the bowl were two olive trees with pipes to transfer the golden oil. The location of the bowl atop the lampstand alludes to the Temple, the site of God's presence.[13] The two olive trees (verse 3) represented the two leaders, Joshua and Zerubbabel, who were anointed by the sacred oil. The rebuilding of the Temple would be accomplished not by human strength but by the power of God's Spirit (verses 6, 7). The mountains of opposition to God's work will be leveled to the ground, and the completion stone will be laid to grace the Temple building.[14] He who had established the foundation of the Temple will carry it to completion. To accomplish this, the leader needed to be in the service of God's Spirit.

It is a statement of faith that God's Spirit can prevail in place of might and power. But the prophetic word will come to pass, its authority vindicated. That is why we should never despise the time of small beginnings (verse 10). The day of joy will come when the last stone that crowns all the work is set in place. The Lord is the source of the authority needed for the completion of the building. Divine light will shine through the Temple and through the worshippers into the community. In the New Testament Jesus Christ is the chief cornerstone in the structure that symbolizes God's kingdom.

In the beginning of chapter 5 the prophet sees an open scroll flying like a banner for all to read. The scroll's dimensions are of giant proportions (Zech. 5:1-3). Like the sun in the sky, the scroll goes out over the whole earth. The scroll is written on both sides like the two tablets of the covenant. The writing contains curses that are the consequences for breaking the covenant. Those who steal and swear falsely will be cut off from the community. God's words act as His agents to accomplish His will and make sure that none escapes His judgments.

In yet another vision the prophet sees an *ephah*, a large container used for measuring grain or flour and comparable to a bushel. As a measuring unit in Scripture, the ephah has connotations of honesty and justice. Here, however, it is connected with evil and injustice in the land (verses 5, 6), because the prophet observes wickedness in its midst. It is personified as a woman who is later carried to Babylon. Without doubt she also represents idolatry. Her removal parallels that of the filthy garments from Joshua the high priest (Zech. 3).

The last vision takes place in the morning, signaling a new era for God's people and the world. The sun rises between two mountains, giving them the color of bronze (Zech. 6:1). The scene reminds one of the two bronze pillars in the Temple (1 Kings 7:13-22).

The first and the last visions have several things in common, such as the imagery of horses and God's presence in the whole earth. The horses come from the direction of sunrise (east) and represent God's army. They serve as guarantees of Judah's peace and rest. "If God's Spirit rested, then so should God's people."[15] Of different colors, the four horses pull "chariots" symbolizing God's active role in the world's history. The four winds of heaven travel over the face of all the earth as God's messenger. Divine dominion extends over all the nations. An angel makes a loud proclamation of worldwide victory and peace.

Zechariah now reports on a new group of exiles that have returned from Babylon with gifts for the needy in the community. Just as Moses used precious metals to build the sanctuary in the wilderness, the prophet is to make two splendid crowns, one for Joshua, the other to be placed in the Temple, perhaps for Zerubbabel. The coronation ceremony takes place in the Temple (Zech. 6:14). The crowns will act as a memorial. Joshua here symbolizes the person called in biblical prophecy the "Branch" (cf. Isa. 4:2) and "the Lord is Our Righteousness." Through Him all sins will be removed. He will build the temple to the Lord and continue David's royal line. As a priest He will sit on His throne. The passage unites in the ministry of the Branch the roles of a priest and a king. The vision presented in this prophecy should shape the moral integrity of the community. God's instructions are to be obeyed.

Sermons About Fasting

In the month of December a delegation from Bethel came to Jerusalem with some questions about fasting days, especially those commemorating the destruction of Jerusalem (Zech. 7:1-3). Zechariah's answer to their questions contains timeless spiritual principles. He first asks about the purpose of fasting (verse 5). Did the judgment not come to Judah because of sins of idolatry? Did justice regulate social relationships in the community? What about loving-kindness mandated by the covenant between God and Israel? The absence of these two virtues had led to the breakdown of social order. Those with power had exploited widows, orphans, and foreigners. Such key moral issues should occupy the minds of those who fast, because the nation came to an end because God's people had rejected such imperatives.

The present generation should learn life lessons from the stubbornness of their predecessors. God's Spirit had moved the prophets who spoke in past history (verse 12). Tragically, the leaders and the people turned a deaf ear to divine instruction. That was why they had been scattered into captivity and their beautiful land devastated. The present custom of fasting must take into consideration such realities. Yet punishment and destruction are never the end of God's story. The Lord's deep feelings for His people manifest themselves as holy jealousy and zeal (Zech. 8:2). Thus He announces

His return to Jerusalem, the city He has always intended to be the dwelling place of righteousness and faithfulness.

Jerusalem will again be called the faithful city and the holy mountain. God's relationship will be restored in righteousness and justice. His promises redefine what is possible to believe. When the new day dawns the city's streets will flow with people of long life. Children playing on the streets will be a sign of blessed family life. The Lord will save His people from sin and all harm. After the renewal of the covenant, God will call them again "my people" (verse 8). He will greatly bless them.

In his second sermon Zechariah summons the people to be strong (verse 9). Insecurity, poverty, and broken relationships characterized the period right after the return from exile. The prophet urges his audience to continue trusting the prophetic word of which he is an instrument. When people call on God, He will hear them. Their prosperity and peace depend on the ways they relate to the Lord and to one another. The rebuilding of the Temple was the result of a complete commitment to God. Even the land has been blessed with abundant produce. God has turned a curse into a great blessing. Someday the divided nation will be reunited and feel strong instead of being afraid.

Based on what the Lord has done for them, the people should speak truth to one another. Acting in the spirit of divine teaching, they can rejoice in the Lord and love truth, peace, and faithfulness. The days of fasting should become times of feasting and joy (verse 19). Mourning should give way to gladness. Love, truth, and peace should govern all relationships. The delegation from Bethel is a sign of the coming of many nations to worship the Lord, and they will admit that "God is with you" (verse 23).

Zechariah ends his sermon with a vision of a glorious future when foreign nations will call on one another to join together in worship of the one true God. Thus they will enter willingly into the new covenant. The initial message of condemnation of the nations (Zech. 1:15; 2:9) has turned into words of blessing and salvation for all humanity that seeks God. His dwelling place in Jerusalem will be the center of the world. Ten persons will take hold of a single Jew, urging him to accompany them to find God (Zech. 8:23).[16] They will demonstrate the strength of their faith by their eagerness to worship the Lord of all.

God's Victorious Intervention

Predictions about Israel's future fill chapters 9 and 10 of Zechariah.

The section announces the long-awaited arrival of the true king (Zech. 9:9, 10), the renewed covenant with God (verses 11, 12), the violent defeat of Israel's enemies, and the rescue of the true people of God (verses 13-17). The prophecy portrays an end-time vision of restoration. The Lord's procession originates in the extreme north, a territory beyond Damascus. He then proceeds south along the coastland, establishing His control over the whole region including Jerusalem. Bringing the Arameans (Syrians) under His control, He puts an end to Tyre's arrogance. The news that the rich city has been burned and its wealth hurled into the sea terrifies the Philistine cities. Their own pride now broken, they become part of the surviving remnant (verses 5-7). They will have a region in Judah like the Jebusites who lived "with the people of Judah in Jerusalem to this day" (Joshua 15:63, NRSV). God is establishing a new order of things, and He will govern it.

The Lord comes to Jerusalem and enters His house (Zech. 9:8-10). The people greet Him as king with shouts of joy (cf. Zeph. 3:14, 15). He is a righteous ruler who humbly rides on a donkey while offering peace and salvation. The Gospel writers refer to this passage when they describe Jesus' triumphant entry into Jerusalem (Matt. 21:5; John 12:15). Zechariah says that Israel's kingdom will again be united and universal peace established. Tools of war will be banished from earth. The king uses His power to set prisoners free from the waterless pit. They will be brought back from places as far away as the ends of the earth (Zech. 9:10, 11). The land will be blessed with an abundance of grain and new wine. God pledges to fulfill His promises because of the blood of the covenant. A double share of joy compensates for past troubles. God's bow and arrows bring Him a worldwide victory. When a great trumpet sounds like thunder, God's flock will shine like the jewels in a crown (verse 16). An abundant supply of blessing will be theirs (Zech. 10:1).

Since God is the Lord of nature, people should ask Him, not diviners, for rain. But at the present moment the people of Israel are like sheep without a shepherd (verse 2). Unfortunately, the shepherds they do have are unfaithful and deserve to be punished (verse 3). The nation lacks good shepherds, so other nations have taken advantage of the situation. The Lord is angry with all of them. The flock is lost and afflicted. The oracle contrasts the divine king with the wicked leaders whom God will punish. Zechariah uses several metaphors to describe strong leaders: they are invincible as a warhorse, steadfast as a cornerstone, reliable as a tent peg, and triumphant as a bow (verses 3, 4). The Lord will be with them. He promises to turn the whole nation into mighty men who will trample their foe underfoot (verse 5). The Lord will save His people and renew His covenant with them. They will increase in number, and He will lead them as His flock.

The prophet announces a great gathering of the captives from everywhere. The Lord will whistle to them, and they will come back (verses 8, 9). He who had scattered them will lead them home from the south (Egypt) and the north (Assyria). Their return will be like the exodus from Egypt. United and strong, God's people will walk in the Lord's name forever, and live with their children. As for proud nations and individuals, God will judge them (Zech. 11:1-3). As tall cedar trees are cut down so will the arrogant and powerful rulers be brought low (cf. Eze. 31) and deprived of their majesty.

Zechariah comes back to the topic of wicked shepherds (Zech. 11:4). Again he criticizes the leaders of Judah for their neglect and abandonment of their flock. Those who tend God's sheep have no mercy on them but lead them to the place of slaughter (cf. Jer. 23:1-8; Eze. 34). They exploit others without mercy and make fortunes through corrupt ways. The Lord instructs Zechariah himself to play the role of a shepherd (Zech. 11:7). He takes two staffs, which represent favor and unity and breaks them, then removes "the three shepherds" (verse 8)[17] and abandons his flock. The snapping of the two staffs means the end of the covenant and the breakup of the nation. It also signals an end to favor and unity. Because of this, others detect and reject the shepherd, then trade him for 30 shekels of silver. The wage is to be cast into the Temple treasury so that the prophet is freed from his obligation. In his place the Lord will raise a new, useless shepherd who will completely abandon the sheep to predators and destruction. In the gospel story Jesus Christ describes Himself as the good Shepherd (John 10). Judas, on the other hand, acts foolishly when he attempts to destroy Jesus, the shepherd of the flock (Matt. 27:7-10).

Zechariah 12 begins with the description of a future battle waged by the nations of the world against Jerusalem. The shift of power takes place when the Lord enters the scene and determines the destiny of the nations, making them drink the cup filled with divine wrath. On that day the Lord promises to strike the enemy's horses with panic and blindness. He will save the tents of Judah, and His Spirit will enable its clans to rule. On the day of the Lord David's dynasty will be linked with the Messenger of the Lord (Zech. 12:10) who will be pierced as Isaac was to have been by Abraham (Gen. 22). The inhabitants of Jerusalem are responsible for piercing

Him. Conscience stricken, they repent and mourn for Him as people did for Josiah king of Judah (see 2 Chron. 35:25). The Messenger's death results in forgiveness of sins, and a fountain in the city will cleanse the people (Zech. 13:1). (The suffering servant in the book of Isaiah [Isa. 53:5, 10] is similarly pierced to death.) The author of Revelation (Rev. 1:7) applies Zechariah 12:10 to Christ's death and His second coming.

Zechariah 13:1-6 predicts the end of all prophecy. First of all, idolatrous leaders are rejected. The same is true of the false prophets whom the members of their own household will punish. Since society now views any prophesying as a form of lying, the penalty for such activity is beating and death. Although the accused person tries to distance himself from the role of a prophet, the scars of the beatings that he has received from his family members now betray him. From the punishment of false prophets, Zechariah next switches to the hostility toward God's shepherd in his "Song of the Sword" (verses 7-9). His humble and helpless sheep suffer and are scattered. Destructive fire annihilates some, but purifies others who call on the Lord's name. The command is given to the sword to attack the shepherd so that the sheep will be scattered. In the light of the New Testament, we can identify the shepherd with Jesus Christ whose suffering and death the biblical prophets foretold.

The last chapter in the book presents another reversal of Jerusalem's fortunes during the Lord's day. It will bring transformations of cosmic proportions. The city first looks almost defeated by a league of nations opposed to God (Zech. 14:1). The enemy divides its spoil until the Lord appears on the Mount of Olives with His angels. An earthquake lifts Jerusalem up, while the hills around become a plain. A way opens east of the city through which the people can escape. The Lord reigns, and the chapter calls Him king three times (verses 9, 16, 17). Night ceases to exist, and eternity begins. Changes in nature result in blessings while the Lord's dominion becomes universal and exclusive. The river flowing from the city brings life, and the trees on its banks bear fruit. The ever-flowing streams of water bring fertility to the whole land. All creatures acknowledge one true God (verse 9). The glory of God dwells in Jerusalem, and the city will never again be depopulated.

Life in the New Jerusalem will be free from any threat of destruction. People will bring plunder from the nations to Jerusalem. The Lord will cause panic among the city's enemies so that they will fight one another. A wasting disease will suddenly strike them (verse 12). In His sermon from the Mount of Olives Jesus said that the way to the future will involve wars and suffering before He comes in glory with His angels. Zechariah says that a plague will strike the nations that refuse to worship God. But the converted nations will honor the Lord and join in an international pilgrimage to Jerusalem as they bring their sacrifices during the Feast of Tabernacles.

God will renew His covenant with His people, and He will be the king of the entire human race. The saved people and their property, such as horses and cooking pots, all become holy to the Lord. Any distinction between the sacred and secular will cease, because everything will be sacred. The divine presence will make all things different.

A man came to a Jewish teacher and said that he would like to pray but did not know how. The rabbi instructed him to talk to God as to a friend. "But I am not sure I can do that either," the man replied.

Then the teacher said, "You can recite the alphabet, can't you? Do that, and the angels will put the letters in their right places and compose a beautiful prayer to God."

Some readers of the Bible have found the last chapters of Zechariah very confusing. When Martin Luther in his study came to chapter 14, he was not sure what the prophet was talking about, so he decided to give up his study of the book. Yet the essence of Zechariah's message seems clear, and we may briefly summarize it as: the Lord is "in control of history and therefore justice will be done. But this just God is one who also freely offers forgiveness."[18] In the end the Messiah will truly accomplish the will of God on earth. Both Israel and the nations will submit themselves to His rule and share in the glorious eternal age. Christ's kingdom will be a universal rule of peace. The people of God will forever enjoy the presence and protection of the One who blesses them.

---

[1] Robertson McQuilkin, *A Promise Kept* (Wheaton, Ill.: Tyndale House, 1998).

[2] No less than 32 different people in the Bible share the name, including the father of John the Baptist (Luke 1).

[3] Some scholars have suggested that we should read Haggai and Zechariah 1-8 as one book.

[4] References to Zechariah in Ezra omit the father's name and call him "son of Iddo" (Ezra 5:1; 6:14, NRSV).

[5] J. Baldwin, *Haggai, Zechariah, and Malachi,* p. 74.

[6] S. Kealy, *An Interpretation of the Twelve Minor Prophets of the Hebrew Bible*, p. 200.

[7] Seventy years equal seven sabbatical years.

[8] Ben C. Ollenburger, "The Book of Zechariah: Introduction, Commentary, and Reflections," *The New Interpreter's Bible* (Nashville: Abingdon, 1996), p. 739.

[9] Zechariah 1:17 uses the word "again" no less than four times.

[10] Ollenburger, p. 761.

[11] Baldwin, p. 114.

[12] The names of Israel's 12 tribes were engraved on the stones worn by the high priest.

[13] Ollenburger, p. 770.

[14] Some scholars think that the great mountain leveled before Zerubbabel (Zech. 4:7-9) is the rubble of the destroyed Temple.

[15] Ollenburger, p. 785.

[16] Baldwin, p. 156: "Ten is used regularly in the Bible as the number of completeness (e.g., Gen. 31:7; Lev. 26:26; Judges 17:10; Ruth 4:2; 1 Sam. 1:8; Jer. 41:8)."

[17] Biblical prophecy often uses the element of three or a third to indicate destruction (for example, Dan. 7:8, 24; Rev. 12:4).

[18] Kealy, p. 217.

Chapter 12

Messages From the Book of Malachi

An idol worshipper once asked a Jewish rabbi, "Where is your God?" The teacher simply answered, "I do not know!"

Then a second question followed: "Teacher, can you see your God?"

"No, I cannot," the rabbi replied. The idol worshipper felt sure that his religion was superior since he knew exactly where his idol was and could see it any time he wished. But it was the teacher who ended the dialogue when he declared, "I cannot see God, but my God can see me!" Some things that an idol can never do are to see, to hear, or to have any feelings toward its worshippers. Since in Malachi's time the people of Judah seemed to have forgotten that their God cared about them, the prophet began his book by engaging them in a dialogue. In this way, he tried to help people overcome their indifference and even apathy toward their spiritual lives.

A contemporary of Ezra and Nehemiah, Malachi lived after the return from Babylonian exile in the middle of the fifth century B.C. His name means "my messenger." Some ancient interpreters have proposed that Malachi was not a personal name but a title for Ezra. "Precisely because we know so little about the human agency through which this word came to us, the word can stand, above all else, as a word of God."[1] The prophet ministered during "an uneventful waiting period, when God seemed to have forgotten His people's enduring poverty and foreign domination in the little province of Judah."[2] The work of rebuilding the Temple had concluded, and sacrificial worship had resumed. It was a period of waiting on God that tested the faith of many. The community was spiritually lukewarm and lacking in moral courage and enthusiasm.

Some of the important issues at that time included a lack of support for the Temple (Mal. 3:8), oppression of the poor (verse 5), and intermarriages with non-Jewish families (Mal. 2:11, 12). "It was a time when the Levites were so poorly supported that they were compelled to work in the fields (Neh. 13:10). People cut grain on the Sabbath while the marketplace was busy as ever (Neh. 13:15-22). It was a period of merciless moneylenders forcing whole families into slavery (Neh. 5:1-5)."[3] The book shows how Judah perverted its covenant relationship with the Lord and corrupted Temple worship. The prophet mentions the challenge to respect the Lord no less than five times.

As he addresses the negative attitude expressed through the people's thoughts and feelings, Malachi casts his message in a formal debate format. He called them back to God, who never changes, and to a renewed and enduring commitment to Him (Mal. 3:6, 7). Furthermore, he defines sin as an act of breaking the covenant. The leaders and the people have become indifferent, bored with service to God, and thus robbed Him of what is due Him. The way they treated their fellow human beings also reflected their negative attitude. They had lost a high view of family life, one resting on a lifelong commitment to one's spouse. Divorce resulting from broken relationships affected society and especially the religious community. The prophet's message challenges so-called nominal or cultural believers. The themes of marriage and divorce and love and election connect his book with Hosea's. The New Testament quotes two passages from Malachi in four different places (Matt.11:10; Mark 1:2; Luke 7:27; Rom. 9:13).

Malachi is the final book of the minor prophets and the last book in the Old Testament. Its 55 verses report six oracles. Forty-seven of those verses are God's first-person speeches. The book intertwines the topics of privilege and responsibility. Also, the theme of God's covenant of love runs throughout the book (Mal. 1:2-5; 4:4). The Lord speaks as Father to Israel His son, implying a living and loving relationship between them. In addition to acting as Father, God is also king and Lord (Mal. 1:6, 14). "The composite picture guards against overfamiliarity on the one hand and a too distant subjection on the other."[4] The Lord invites people to respect Him and walk with Him (Mal. 2:6).

God's dominion extends beyond Israel's borders (Mal. 1:5), so that in the end all the nations will get to know and worship Him by bringing choice offerings (Mal. 1:14; 3:12).

The Lord will execute His judgment from the Temple (Mal. 3:1-5). On the great and terrible day of the Lord (Mal. 4:5) the righteous will be refined while fire will consume the wicked. The book ends with a look back at Moses and forward to the return of Elijah. The mention of the two prophets (verses 4-6) in the book's concluding verses sums up God's prophetic revelation given through many previous centuries. This collection of sacred texts looks forward to the complete fulfillment of the purpose for which they were written. A Jewish tradition claims that when Haggai, Zechariah, and Malachi died, the Holy Spirit left Israel—the reason some interpreters have called Malachi "the seal of the prophets."

The God of Love

The literal meaning of the first word in Malachi's book is "burden." The word of the Lord weighs heavy on the prophet's heart and mind, and he needs to deliver it so that the people can prepare for the events to come. The use of the name Israel in Malachi 1:1 indicates that the revelation concerns all who belong to the nation. Malachi affirms God's constant love and compassion for His people (verse 2). These two qualities are the basis of the coming renewal. God's words "I have loved you" remind one of a similar statement found in Jeremiah 31:3. As strong as God's love is, there are always some who find it difficult to accept. So Malachi points to the early evidence of their election by God in the time of the patriarchs. Israel's continued existence is proof of the Lord's unchanging love. Esau was Jacob's twin brother and the slightly older of the two. The Lord's preference for Jacob came out of pure love.

The words "I hated Esau" (Mal. 1:3) mean that God did not select him for a special purpose as He did with Jacob. To "hate" in this case means to love less. The rejection of Esau did not have to do with his wrongdoings but with God's absolute freedom to choose whom He wants. Thus God's choice of Jacob to be His covenant partner was a free and undeserved gift. Yet it involved important responsibilities. Since the people did not live up to them, God had to apply severe discipline. Before Malachi's time the Edomite territory located southeast of the Dead Sea had come under the control of a desert people called Nabateans who later built their capital of Petra. Thus by suffering a defeat, the Edomites also experienced divine discipline. In some places in the Bible Edom stands for the non-Hebrew nations.

Unlike the remnant of Judah, the Edomites were not privileged to return to their land and rebuild its ruined cities and villages (verse 4). Because of God's anger, the land of Edom would remain desolate. Malachi is telling the people of Judah to rejoice in their God-given privileges and stop complaining. Although Israel's history was not free from trouble, when compared with the experiences of other nations, it was still evident that God had been exceptionally good toward the chosen people. They needed to open their eyes and see the divine providence at work in their history.

Malachi, as God's messenger, speaks with divinely given authority to the priests whom he calls the Lord's messengers (verse 6; cf. 2:7). Entrusted with great responsibilities they were especially accountable for what they were doing. Sadly, they failed to obey their Father and Master.[5] They broke the relationship of love and trust with the Lord by presenting to Him deficient sacrifices. Unworthy and polluted offerings that came from unclean hearts dishonored God's name and made the Lord's table despised by the officiating priests (Mal. 1:7). A human governor would not accept blemished goods, yet they presented God with blind, lame, and sick animals in spite of the clear prohibitions not to do so (Ex. 12:5; Lev. 1:3). The expectation of God's favor of grace goes together only with acceptable sacrifices (Mal. 1:9). He takes no pleasure in empty worship. To shut the door to the Temple is preferable to worthless offerings that lead to false confidence. The Lord's rejection of sacrifices meant the repudiation of the people.

God's universal reign stretches from the rising of the sun to its setting (verse 11). He accepts praises originating from every sincere heart. Divine grandeur surpasses the greatness of the Temple. This fact prepares the way for the nations to come to know God and honor Him with a worldwide worship. Their "pure offerings" will surpass in quality all previous ones. It is through worship that the Gentiles will be reconciled with God and claim His promises. Some scholars maintain that the text is eschatological and refers to the messianic age.

The present worship in the Temple falls short of divine ideals (verses 12, 13) and is blind to the vision of a glorious future. Malachi criticizes the dichotomy between worship and everyday life, between praise and service. He says that pride and violence should give place to faith and repentance. The priests should be the first to demonstrate such a change. Vows or promises to God are meant to be kept. To break a vow was a very serious offense that could result in a curse.[6] God's people should learn a lesson in faithfulness taught by foreigners whose trust in God resulted in many blessings.

Like other biblical prophets, Malachi now addresses the priests and the Levites who served in the temple (Mal. 2:1; cf. Hosea 5:1; Amos 3:1; Micah 1:2). They had a special covenant relation with God (Jer. 33:20, 21). Their income consisted of tithes and offerings that depended on the harvests. The covenant with Levi was one of peace and based on deep reverence for God (Mal. 2:5).[7] God had entrusted the priests in Israel with knowledge of the Torah (Deut. 17:9; 33:10). They were teachers who dispensed instruction through the preaching and teaching of the sacred texts (Mal. 2:7). For Malachi, the priest was the Lord's messenger (cf. Isa. 42:19) to the people. The correct handling of God's instruction rested on the teacher's integrity. Each had to set an example in word and deed by walking with the Lord in righteousness and leading others away from sin.

A decline in the priests' high calling causes others to stumble in their own ways. Malachi 2:8 shows the power of influence. The sins of the priests consisted of inferior offerings and faulty teaching. The prophet says that the Lord despised as much the sacrifice in the Temple as the dung that makes people and their offerings unclean (verse 3). God would remove the wicked priests so as to preserve the covenant. The prophet's passionate words indicate his feelings toward the blatant abuses by the priests. Another punishment for the duplicity and hypocrisy of the priests would be that the common people would despise them (verse 9). Malachi taught that persons who fail to honor God's name (Mal. 1:6) would themselves be despised and rejected by others.

"Return to Me!"

The whole nation of Israel was one family in God's eyes, just as were their ancestors when they went down to Egypt during the time of the patriarchs. The father of the nation was Jacob whom Malachi mentions in three more places in the book (Mal. 1:2; 2:12; 3:6). The Creator-God was also Israel's Parent who taught them how to walk (cf. Hosea 11:1). But the breaking of promises in business and family relations shattered the concept of brotherhood. In particular, marriages with people from different religious groups undermined Israel's spiritual life (Mal. 2:11). Infidelity and divorce eroded the stability of the community. The problem at stake with mixed marriages was idolatry. Thus the issue was not race but religion. Rahab, Ruth, and other foreigners forsook their gods and committed themselves to the Lord. Worship of idols among God's people, on the other hand, led to captivity in Assyria and Babylon. Mere shedding of tears would not change the inevitable course of events (verse 13).

Men divorced their Hebrew wives so that they could marry foreign women for social or material purposes. Ezra taught that foreign gods polluted God's sanctuary because of such intermarriages with non-Jewish nations (Ezra 9:1, 2). The same also profaned God's people. Children and grandchildren born of such unions would lack blessings (Mal. 2:12). On the other hand, a couple's individual loyalty to the covenant God would ensure lasting companionship between the partners (cf. verse 14). Stable marriages come from mutual loyalty and faithfulness. But the prophet says that these very traits were now absent. Trust between the spouses provides the security so needed for the healthy growth of the children. That is why Malachi entreats men to remain true to the wives of their youth.

Since God hates divorce (verse 16), He desires faithfulness to marriage vows (as demonstrated by the story of Hosea and Gomer [Hosea 1-3]). Both individual lives and the community depend on the marriage principle. The Lord will defend the wives' positions and punish the faithless husbands. This passage anticipates the teaching about divorce presented in the New Testament. Malachi wonders, just as Habakkuk did, how long God will delay to fulfill His promises (Mal. 2:17). The people doubted and questioned both the love (Mal. 1:2) and justice (Mal. 2:17) of the Lord. It is clear that God is just (Isa. 30:18), but the people complain that they have not actually experienced it from Him. In fact, the wicked prosper and enjoy blessings in spite of all the evil they do. But the coming day of the Lord will bring justice.

Through Malachi the Lord announces the coming of His messenger (Mal. 3:1) who will be God's herald to prepare the processional way for the arrival of a great king (cf. Ex. 23:20; Isa. 40:3). In Bible times this task belonged to the prophet.[8] For example, Moses in the wilderness prepared the way for the Lord's appearance on Mount Sinai. Now the Lord will suddenly come to His Temple. The "See, I am sending . . ." (Mal. 3:1, NRSV) matches the "See I will send . . ." of Malachi 4:5 that identifies the messenger as the prophet Elijah who never died but was translated to heaven. Jerome regarded the messenger of the covenant as John the Baptist, while the Lord coming to the Temple was Jesus the Savior.

A test of faithfulness will follow the Lord's coming. The prophet wonders who can pass it (Mal. 3:2). Yet it leads not to destruction but to refining and purification. Other prophets also describe the time of trial as an opportunity to purify the character and remove all impurity (Isa. 1:25; Jer. 6:29; Eze. 22:17-22). The Levites will be purified so that they will be able to present acceptable offerings in the future. Ordinary people who are purified will be as holy as the descendants of Levi. Their offerings will be accepted by the Lord who will take pleasure in them. But the same test will bring destruction on unrepentant sorcerers, liars, adulterers, and all who take advantage of widows, orphans, and foreigners (Mal. 3:5). As for the

Lord, His love for His people never changes (verses 6, 7). He is consistent in His dealings with human beings. His constant goodness and love call people to repentance.

The Lord had decreed that 10 percent of all income belongs to Him (Lev. 27:30). Not to give what belongs to Him is considered an act of robbery (Mal. 3:8). Israel used the offerings to support those who ministered in the sanctuary. Even the Levites who worked in the Temple were expected to pay tithes (Num. 18:25-29). Nehemiah pointed to the people's failure to pay tithes (Neh. 10:39; 13:11). God abundantly blesses those who are generous in giving (Prov. 11:24), for He loves a cheerful giver (2 Cor. 9:7). In Malachi 3:10 God challenges people to test Him. When they honor Him by bringing food to His house, He will pour through the windows of heaven as many blessings as the amount of rain that fell on earth during the great Flood (cf. Gen. 7:11). Such blessings will signify that the God of justice is still among His people. Moreover, the Lord will also protect their goods from devourers such as locusts (Mal. 3:11). Spiritual blessings will accompany the material blessings.

The prophet now returns to the current situation in the land. The presence of injustice in society discourages any attitude of integrity. The Lord has heard complaints about this and has decided to act (cf. Gen. 18:20). "The people are given their lengthiest, but final, chance to speak."[9] They wonder if it really pays to obey God's commands and be repentant and humble (Mal. 3:14). But those who commit crimes test God's patience. Envying the arrogant was a constant temptation to the godly (cf. Ps. 73:2-14). How should the righteous view such inequality and oppression? Malachi answers that the righteous persons live in the light of God's final judgment on the day when the wrongs will be made right. It means that God cares and sees everything (Mal. 3:16).

The faithful members of the community who trust in the Lord should encourage one another with this message of hope and comfort. God has written their names in a special book (cf. Ex. 32:32; Ps. 69:28; Dan. 12:1), called here "the scroll of remembrance." The Lord will never forget any act of faithfulness. The title "my treasured possession" is a privilege of the highest order (Mal. 3:17) normally applied to the whole nation of Israel (Ex. 19:5; Deut. 7:6; 26:18; Ps. 135:4). Here the prophet reserves the expression for individual members of the faithful remnant. The righteous serve or worship God, and His parental care and love spares them from destruction. The names of the righteous are already written before God, but they will be revealed on the day when the Lord will act and appear as "the sun of righteousness" with healing in His wings (Mal. 4:2).

The fire that refines (Mal. 3:2) is also the same fire that can destroy. The prophet compares the judgment day to a vast hot oven that will reduce arrogant and evildoers to ashes (Mal. 4:1). But God will spare those who respect and honor His name from the all-consuming blaze (verses 2, 3). To them the "Rising Sun" will not bring destruction but healing. (In the Bible the sun is a symbol for God [Ps. 84:11].) They will go out and leap for joy as they bask in the sunlight shed by the Sun of Righteousness. At last they will enjoy freedom from the wicked oppressors who are no more.

Malachi's book closes with an affirmation of God's past revelation. The command to remember Him and His Torah is one of the most important exhortations in the Bible (Mal. 4:4). Not to remember God and His law given to Moses and other prophets is an act of sin. Just as in the past Moses set the stage for God's coming at Sinai, so will Elijah prepare the way before the great and terrible day of the Lord. Elijah was a great prophet who never experienced death. He will come to restore all things, beginning with reconciliation among close family members (verse 6). The rebellion of children against their parents causes social chaos (Micah 7:6). Yet God's original plan was that home would be the place where people read, explained, and lived His Word. The rejection of God's revelation will result in a curse on earth.

The references to Moses and Elijah in the concluding section are a fitting introduction to the Gospel of Matthew in which the two appear and converse with Jesus on the Mount of Transfiguration (Matt. 17). Jews reserve an empty seat, an extra drink, and an open door for Elijah whenever they celebrate Passover, in the expectation that Elijah will someday come back.[10] The Gospels, however, apply the prophecy about Elijah to the ministry of John the Baptist, who prepared the way for Jesus the Messiah. After Jews read Malachi 4:5, 6 in the synagogue, they repeat verse 4 so that it ends on a positive note. Yet even though verses 5 and 6 appear harsh, we can take them as a divine promise that ties the beginning of Malachi's book with its end: because the Lord loves His people (Mal. 1:2) He promises to send His messenger to warn them before that great and terrible day. Then God will not have to curse the earth, but grace it with eternal blessings.

Confucius, the famous teacher and philosopher from China, once said: "Heaven means to be one with God." In a similar way Ellen White summed up the blessings of the eternal life in the following words:

"The nations of the saved will know no other law than the law of heaven. All will be a happy, united family, clothed with the garments of praise and thanksgiving. Over the scene the morning stars will sing together, and the sons of God will shout for joy, while God and Christ will unite in proclaiming, 'There shall be no more sin, neither shall there be any more death.'"[11]

---

[1] Eileen M. Schuller, "The Book of Malachi: Introduction, Commentary, and Reflections," *The New Interpreter's Bible* (Nashville: Abingdon Press, 1996), vol. 7, p. 853.

[2] J. Baldwin, *Haggai, Zechariah, and Malachi*, p. 211.

[3] S. Kealy, *An Interpretation of the Twelve Minor Prophets of the Hebrew Bible*, p. 227.

[4] Baldwin, p. 217.

[5] The words "servant" and "son" appear in parallelism when King Ahaz said to his Assyrian lord: "I am your servant and your son" (2 Kings 16:7, NRSV).

[6] The word for curse here is the same one God used in Genesis 3 when He cursed the serpent and the ground.

[7] "A covenant of peace" was promised to Phinehas who was a descendant of Levi (Num. 25:10-13).

[8] The Bible uses the titles "prophet" and "messenger" interchangeably (2 Chron. 36:15, 16; Isa. 42:19; Haggai 1:13).

[9] Schuller, p. 872.

[10] Kealy, p. 239.

[11] Ellen G. White, *Prophets and Kings*, pp. 732, 733.